Published by Dana Press, a Division of The Charles A. Dana
Foundation, Incorporated

**DANA
PRESS**

The Charles A. Dana Foundation
505 Fifth Avenue, Sixth Floor
New York, NY 10017

DANA is a federally registered trademark.

Printed in the United States of America

ISBN-13: 978-1-932594-58-4

Library of Congress Control Number: 2013957109

Cover design and layout by Leslie Hanson

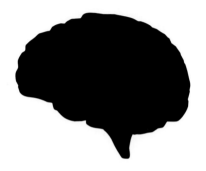

YOU'VE GOT SOME
EXPLAINING TO DO

Advice for Neuroscientists Writing for Lay Readers

JANE NEVINS

TABLE OF CONTENTS

INTRODUCTION

IN MARCH 2013, Harvard psychologist Steven Pinker joined satirist Fran Lebowitz for a conversation before a sold-out audience at the Rubin Museum of Art in New York City. In due course, their discussion arrived at academic writing, which Lebowitz complained was "like trying to read cement." Pinker, a famous exception to that criticism, fended off her shot with a point he makes often in talks and essays about academic writing for general readers: what he calls "the curse of knowledge," which he describes as the difficulty of going "back in your mind to the state you were in before you knew something and explain[ing] it to others."

Thus spoke a sympathetic writer who, as a scholar, knows this dilemma close-up. If you're in the predicament he described, believe me: lay editors feel your pain, too, but we look at it a little differently—as a practical matter of solving problems that we see scientists wrestle with, or not notice, in writing about their science for lay readers. The idea behind this book is to help you so that you can solve or avoid most of these problems yourself. Some of them are ridiculously simple to fix. Others take a mental workout that (like a real workout) is easier for some than others to get used to. Solving those problems boils down to thinking differently, when writing lay science, from the way you think when writing for peers. Don't worry: since both lay and scientific writing have good reasons for being as they are, this book is not an attack on your peer-writing habits. Rather, its intention is to offer the reasons and information that can help you adopt other habits—and be successful and happy with the lay-writing task you have in mind.

YOU AND YOUR READER

The first part of this book is about you and your reader, because writing is, in effect, a conversation. Having a clear sense of whom you're talking with and what you're talking about is critical. That's why I called this part "The Meet-up." The goal is to enable you to think about where the story you have in mind, and the way you expect to write it, meet up with your reader. What you and the reader want has to be clear to you before you start, especially if you hate rewriting (which you should not!). And these wants aren't necessarily the same.

SIMPLE FIXES

In our high school and college writing classes we were told, "Write conversationally." We understood that didn't mean reproducing conversation's shortcuts, bad grammar, and sentence fragments; most of us interpreted the old advice as, "Write like you talk, but in complete sentences." Lucky for editors, writers following this advice produce a feast of writing flaws, most because they forget the nonverbal dimensions of conversation. Because language can either blur or supply that dimension, Part Two discusses common usage practices that muddle or sharpen your writing. Thankfully, bad usage habits are painless to break, and good ones are intrinsically rewarding. If you already have a first draft, you can vet it for usage and almost certainly make it better.

SCIENCE AND STYLE

Part Three is about instances when, for a while at least, you may be at odds with communication habits tagging along from your science life. Deciding what your reader may need to have explained is one part of it. Another part is how a lay reader is processing your words. Still another part is keeping in mind why you think the reader wants to know what you have to say. It sounds like a lot of intuiting, imagining, and guessing—whatever you'd like to call it—beyond the obvious work of gathering, organizing, and writing the content. You must wonder how you can do this while still achieving momentum and flow in the writing. But it's a little like dancing once you've called the tune: after you get going, you remember the moves, and you handle it.

WHERE THIS ADVICE COMES FROM

The Dana Foundation's Dana Press began in 1990 with a lay-oriented newsletter, *BrainWork*, and grew to publish other periodicals and general interest books about the brain in print and electronic formats. As editor in chief, I got to edit scientists' writing for lay readers for nearly twenty-five years, and the advice here comes from that experience. But if the writing commitment you've made is your maiden voyage in writing for lay readers, you might be encouraged by a different fact about my background.

I was a writer and newspaper editor who took a consulting assignment to launch and write *BrainWork* with the help of three scientific advisors: Maxwell Cowan, Floyd Bloom, and Lewis Judd. Without them, the publication would have been dead on arrival. (Actually, the prototype issue *was* dead; they hated it.) I had had both zero scientific training and a science-free career. I call *Brainwork*'s first year my yearlong migraine. But with a degree of patience that still amazes me, the advisors explained, suggested, named names, and dispatched me to interview (and reinterview) constellations of scientists. Sure, I knew where readers would be coming from with regard to the brain, but I had to learn as much as I could about the scientists' perspective. Once I could understand what they did and cared about, it was possible to plow a path to common ground, to see convergent points of interest, and to get the science and the reader onto the same page. Thus, my challenge was like yours now, just in reverse. And if I could do it, I have no doubt you can, too.

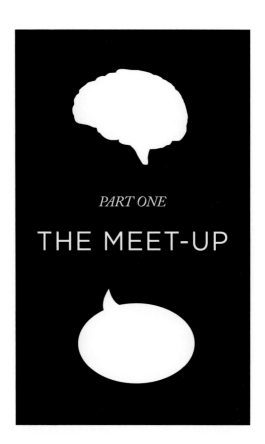

PART ONE

THE MEET-UP

INTRODUCTION

IF you're composing an inquiry to editors that predicts, "This [article/book/blog] will be read by general educated readers as well as scientists, physicians, students, anthropologists, sociologists, psychiatrists, lawyers, and philosophers," stop right there.

Thinking of all the professionals for whom a subject may come up and considering them prospective readers is a natural mistake, but it really is a mistake. Your subject—something involving brain science—is only what readers notice when flipping through a magazine, surfing online, or browsing a bookstore. It will pique their interest, of course. But what makes them readers or nonreaders is the perspective you're offering.

Perspective is not your subject, but rather how you plan to approach it. Planning to show that a particular phenomenon in brain science is amazing and beautiful means you will engage one kind of reader, while planning to show the same topic as a reason for healthy behavior means you'll engage another kind. And the details and ideas needed to show each perspective are different.

If you are at the stage where you have just realized you know some unique or exciting science that you feel nonscientists would love to know about, then you have to do some thinking to bring that intuition to the surface. You'll have to ask, "What in this science has me wanting to tell nonscientists about it? How would I steer the conversation if I were to meet up with potential readers?" In other words, you need to put your finger on the perspective animating you and making you confident of its interest to a lay reader.

If you already know what your perspective will be, then it's possible to form a sense of your reader, because you know, more or less, what sort of person would start or respond to a conversation from that perspective in a social setting. That's the same sort of person who will be reading what you're thinking of writing.

The idea of writing as a conversation with another person is more than a metaphor; it's a reality. You literally can't write anything without thinking of who will be reading it. Even notes to yourself are for someone who will later read them; that someone just happens to be you. Understanding that writing is a conversation is practical as well, because it affects what you write. It means that when discussing your perspective with this reader, you'll bring up some things and not others, and you'll adjust your writing voice, too.

Getting your perspective, your reader, and your voice squared away is the mental workout I mentioned in the Introduction. Think of it, maybe, as another analogy: training for a distance run. Getting in shape might not make the run a snap, but it does make it easier.

1
THINKING ABOUT
YOUR READER

THE times are good to write about the brain. Readers are multiplying, and all kinds of perspectives are attracting them. To name just a few of the latter: how findings in brain research relate to readers' health, nutrition, or longevity; the brain-health considerations involving how they spend their time, do their jobs, rear their children, and make choices in their lives; the brain's role in economics, in creativity, in professional sports, and in experiencing culture and entertainment; how brain research fits into justice, public policy, war, and progress in developing countries; and the personal and societal ethical issues brain science raises. The science you're thinking of writing about may inform any of these areas of life, and the great rise in interest means that someone is already curious about your topic.

This happy state of affairs also means that prospective lay readers' interests are more diverse than ever, which makes necessary a rude-sounding question that editors often ask authors: "Who do you think will read this?" Especially in the case of brain science, where details can become arcane very fast, it's important to have a clear idea about your reader. Whose interest meshes not only with your general subject, but also with what you plan to say about it?

For example, let's say you study brain development and plan

to write about how play influences children's brains and at what ages. Parents, grandparents, teachers, and people who simply find children or play interesting will want to know how skills and cognition develop, which studies demonstrate it, and, perhaps, how they can take advantage of the findings in simple, concrete ways. Special-education professionals, child psychologists, and pediatricians will be looking for more analysis of the findings and, if not causal claims, at least closely reasoned correlations that they might consider fitting into their professional practices. Public or school officials, game designers, playground-equipment makers, and other long-term planners will expect good analysis, too, but they will look to understand where the research is leading and how they should be prepared to follow. Lastly, other scientists, as well as students, will be hungry to know how the nitty-gritty of the findings informs their own research. To start writing with blissful confidence that you know enough about your subject to please *all* these readers is a trap. None of them wants to know everything you know.

As an analogy, imagine being at a social gathering. Someone—say, a lawyer—asks you a question about memory. You're about to answer, but another guest, who happens to be a scientist, has heard the question and steps over to see what you'll say. How do you handle this? What will be interesting to the lawyer will be old news to the scientist. And heaven forfend if the other scientist has published on this and could be critical of your answer. But if you try to craft your answer to gratify both listeners, odds are that one or both will soon drift away, one bored and the other befuddled. That happens with readers, too, if they realize that you aren't quite talking to them—that you're looking over your shoulder at someone else.

In other words, consciousness of everything you know will

be a burden on a coherent story line unless you first consult yourself about the story you want to tell—and the way of handling it that is formed or half-formed in your mind—and then envision the reader most likely to soak it up. Having your intentions and your reader clearly in mind is a compass. Some content will be obvious, other content out of the question, and the tone and language to use will be evident. Having determined your audience, you've reduced your problem to just writing well. And when you write well, readers can surprise you.

Consider Princeton psychologist Daniel Kahneman, the 2002 Nobel laureate in economics for his pioneering work in economic decision making. After publishing five academic books and hundreds of studies over decades, he wrote his first book for lay readers, *Thinking, Fast and Slow*, published in 2011. His Introduction begins this way:

> *Every author, I suppose, has in mind a setting in which readers of his or her work could benefit from having read it. Mine is the proverbial office water-cooler, where opinions are shared and gossip is exchanged. I hope to enrich the vocabulary that people use when they talk about the judgments and choices of others, the company's new policies, or a colleague's investment decisions.*

Not surprisingly, the book quickly appeared on the *Wall Street Journal's* business-book best-seller list. But it also sped to the top of all the general nonfiction lists. It even won fans among neuroscientists without mentioning the brain (it's between the lines throughout). Why? By choosing his goal (a clear lay account of decision making) and envisioning the reader he expected to appreciate it most, he produced a discussion that was richly informative for people both more and less sophisticated than those he had in mind.

Here's the point: You may not have a Nobel (yet), but, like Kahneman, you have an expanse of knowledge ranging in description from extraordinarily specialized to understandable by anyone. So, Kahneman's evocation of the "setting" he envisioned is worth a second look. He described early- or midcareer business readers with solid reasons to think about decision making. He wasn't ruling out any reader, but rather appointing in his mind's eye the conversation partner for his subject—the reader most likely to welcome and use it—and trusting the intelligence of others to read it, too, if they happened to see a benefit. You'll have to appoint your conversation partner, as well, but before you can, you have to be sure you know what you're going to write about.

2
THINKING ABOUT
YOUR SUBJECT

EVEN if you can envision readers for any aspect of your subject area, you're on the road to executing a data dump if you start writing sure of only that much.

You first have to pin down the perspective that stimulated your decision to write about the subject and look forward to laying it out. You should believe that your perspective will be different from and more interesting than what has already been published about the subject, and, I hope, find yourself thinking of it out of the blue. It sounds a bit like pop psychology, doesn't it? It's not. Writing is hard work, and motivation matters.

Being energized about your take on the subject is also practical: when you're down in the weeds of the details, you work your way out by remembering the point of the effort. It is also practical to know that your idea is original or different, because you want an editor to share your enthusiasm, and an editor's first question is always whether or how an idea is new.

At the same time, some things signal problems ahead if you push on without more thought. Two red flags are common. One is that a writer's idea tends to keep shifting; the other is that a proposed article or book doesn't really light the writer up. In either case, it usually turns out that the writer started thinking about a project for the wrong reasons or the idea is simply too vague or general.

OUGHT VERSUS WANT

More often than you might guess, accomplished people start working on an article or a book because they feel they ought to do it, not because they particularly want to do it. Some have been lobbied by friends who are proud of them. Others have been approached by editors who have read about them or seen them interviewed. Occasionally, an author feels duty bound to correct a misconception that's getting too widespread, or has pioneered a subject and is tired of seeing it written about badly. Once in a rare while, a distinguished and otherwise sane scientist will decide it's time to pay back critics whose carping on the way up still hurts. But most of the time, the scientist in an "ought" frame of mind about writing simply feels that it's important to help the lay public keep up with the research. None of these motives is ideal for developing a project, but some are worse than others.

Editors regularly reject projects inspired by negative motives, because they're rarely good reading. An author's feelings unavoidably shape his or her writing, and as a result, a negative motive tends to show—in content, in the form of too much text devoted to what is wrong and too little to what is right, and in style, in the form of condescension, preachiness, irritability, or mean-spiritedness. Editors do understand the importance of fixing misconceptions or mopping up after sloppy publications, but a writer trying to do that has to show us a piece full of good information that either ignores the bad information or corrects it gently. We also understand (very well) the sting of a critic's attack, but most manuscripts we see trying to respond are at best, defensive, and at worst, unbecoming. When discussing a project with a writer who is troubled by other points of view, I always say, "Get it out of your system, write it just the way you're saying, and then hit the delete key." If I want to publish you, it's because you have valuable things to say. Critics and lesser stuff out there really aren't interesting.

The well-meant motives are better—at least they get you to take the plunge—but often they make writing feel like a chore: if you write to please your friends, you may find your content and style choices driven by their knowledge, tastes, and reasons for urging you to write, rather than a clear sense of what you would like to say to your intended reader. If an editor has brought you a specific idea that you wouldn't have proposed yourself and you go ahead with it anyway, your imagination and intuition may hit the snooze button, leaving you to plod on with your intellect alone. The best of the positive reasons—writing to commit a public service—presents a paradox: you get a good result when you are selfish and take your favorite angle on your subject, whereas simply deciding to educate the public is a little like writing a check for a worthy cause; emotional distance from the task may result in an unimaginative product.

The one exception among positive "ought" reasons is an offer you can't refuse, such as an op-ed approach from the *New York Times*, a steady gig on WebMD, or a six-figure book contract. Such opportunities should help you make the leap from "ought" to "want" in a hurry, and not just because they mean large and well-defined audiences. One incentive that leads publishers to approach a scientist is respect. If the feeling is mutual, you should be able to work with the editor to secure as much freedom in handling the project as if you had proposed it to the publisher, instead of the other way around.

NAILING THE PERSPECTIVE

One of the oddest things about writing is how often a final

product turns out to be richer than, or less centered on, the idea the writer began with. The reason is simple: the process of writing tends to clarify the challenges of the idea as it starts taking shape in words.

Therein lies a dilemma related to getting published. The writer's perspective—the argument to be made, the question that an expository story will address, the way the information will be handled—carries more weight than writing style when an editor first considers a proposed article or book. Moreover, the editor wants to see the idea in a query or an overview first, without having to read the entire manuscript. That means settling the concept down, trying to nail it, despite knowing it may change somewhat once the writing is under way.

Trust me: whatever you think you'd like to write, it's probably a lot vaguer than it seems when merely thinking about it, and the type of angle you expect to pursue may not even square with the content you envision. What I mean is, if you'd like to write about, for example, child brain development in a way that parents will read, but the content you keep thinking about is all biology and no behavior, there's a gap you'll have to close. In short, you have to start to articulate your perspective, one way or another, to make your idea concrete and spot any conceptual problems with it.

Some writers make headway with perspective by testing it on friends, talking about the idea and how they plan to lay it out, and prodding them for a reaction. That works if you talk to lay people like those who you expect will want to read the piece, colleagues who have written successfully for lay readers, or the editor who has invited you to write. But you'll have to stop talking and start writing at some point, so it is quickest and most effective to just get going.

Many writers (I'm one of them) have to plunge right into a first draft, more or less spewing all the clever and random thoughts that deserve to be in the piece. (Remember Ronald Reagan's quip about the kid cleaning the stable because he was sure there was a pony somewhere in there?) In my case, I may write for many days before I think I've figured out what I want to get across and what specifics I'll bring up. Then I junk whatever rough outline I started with and do another to better organize the direction I've found emerging. That approach isn't for everybody, because it's time consuming and even depressing if the thing doesn't come together with nearly the same élan as it seemed to have.

Other writers suss out their perspective by drafting a query or overview, often writing several versions before one finally looks like the story they want to write. Another technique is to start drafting pieces of specific content and shuffling them around to see how they line up as a story. And finally, some writers can make their perspective concrete enough to guide a first draft by writing a few descriptive sentences of the kind you see in magazine tables of contents or in brief book reviews.

DITCH THOSE LECTURE NOTES

However you go about formulating your perspective, pulling it out of your academic lecture notes is not a good idea. Editors often receive queries from scholars proposing to adapt a popular lecture for publication to lay readers. We usually say thanks, but no thanks, because the academic priorities served by lectures are rarely the same as the priorities for the general reader.

Some subjects reliably interest lay readers, and, as a result, writers, editors, and publishers have typical ways—formulas, if you will—of presenting those subjects. These lead to the niches that I'll describe in the next chapter. But overlaying all the niches is one critical reality that many scientist-authors underestimate or forget: general readers are leisure readers. They read because they want to, not because they have to.

An October 2010 article by Abe Peck in *Pacific Standard* magazine discusses a then-newly published, decade-long study by Northwestern University's Readership Institute. The researchers surveyed 37,000 people about 74,000 online and print articles and how the readers engaged with or disengaged from the articles. In the responses and in hundreds of follow-up interviews, the researchers identified more than forty kinds of "experiences." Experiences of engaged readers were, for example, "kick back and wind down," "makes me smarter," "my reward for doing other things," "talk about and share," "utilitarian," and "I lose myself in the pleasure of reading this magazine." Experiences that caused readers to disengage included "negativity," "sameness," "disappoints me," and "overload."

One example that Peck discussed further was *Popular Science* magazine, which has 1.3 million readers. The study found that *Popular Science* readers engage with the magazine as a "timeout experience," he wrote, and he quoted the *Popular Science* editor's reaction: "Hearing people tell us that this was a leisure activity and not an educational tool reminded us to, for instance, make sure we weren't using jargon . . . not let our infographics get too ambitious. If any of our content feels like too much work to figure out, or makes the reader feel dumb, you suddenly shatter that 'escape sensation.'"

Happily, the findings of the study did put to rest two clichés you often hear about lay readers: that you must come up with some way they can apply the science, and that science has to be dumbed down for them. Still, it is important to always remember that general readers—even those who read to become smarter—have different interests from academic readers when it comes to the kind of detail and perspective you choose for your subject.

3
WHAT READERS WANT

STEVEN Pinker's idea, mentioned in the introduction, of writing for lay readers under a "curse of knowledge" is vivid, but it's a little like someone in the economic top 1 percent complaining about the curse of wealth. On that analogy, setting out on a lay-writing project means you take the Ford instead of the limo. The real question is which portfolio to tap for what you write, and that's often an exciting decision to make.

However, Pinker's description of the task—one in which you "go back in your mind to the state you were in before you knew something and explain it to others"—seems unhelpful. (I say that respectfully, since it's hard to argue with success.) Most likely, when you became interested in science, you were in a state of infatuation and determination to learn everything about it, while what infatuated others led them to become lawyers, businesspeople, teachers, artists, clergy, athletes, public officials, yoga instructors, and so on. So going back to an ignorant version of yourself means you might not meet up with your reader at all; you might just meet yourself. I would rather describe the task as writing for another adult who is interested in knowing your perspective on a science-related question. That, too, is exciting, because it means more ideas to be shared and sets clear boundaries for handling any technical points that need to be explained.

Here's the paradigm: You want to write something for a particular reason, and your reader wants to read it for the same reason. It's not about all the science you know, but about the science that fits your and the reader's attraction to the story. Believe this, and it will lighten your task by orders of magnitude, because you can focus on choosing the appropriate scientific content and making it clear and interesting.

Since people read different things for various reasons, you need to see in the crowd the reader who fits your writing intention—the one you easily imagine on the other side of the author-reader conversation, the one who engages with what you plan to write the way you're going to write it. One way to start picturing that is to consider what publishers think they know about their readers.

The categories that follow are a kind of editor-bird's-eye view of readers. Magazines have long profiled subscribers for marketing and advertising purposes, and online publishers now do similar analyses, although the data are a little thin in some areas. The book industry has never had good reader statistics and depends largely on experience with titles well or poorly received (e-book data gathering will surely change that). Nevertheless, book publishers and booksellers use categories to adorn book jackets and to group titles in stores—they call them niches—and their ideas about readers in those niches are similar to the more systematic analyses conducted by other publishers.

Niches are types of content and presentation that attract a significant body of readers. Editors are niche-minded about science-related manuscripts, because it is an easy way to guess if subscribers or book customers will like a project. Considering such categories is useful to you as an author, because seeing how your planned project relates to their characteristics and demographics can help you stay on course (when you think you've got the "curse") and help you remember your reader.

GENERAL EDUCATED READERS

When querying editors about potential articles or books, scientists often say that their proposed work is "for general educated readers." By this, they usually mean that they plan to use nontechnical language and have assumed that well-educated readers will read about the science as long as it is well explained. But "gerries," as legendary late editor Joyce Engelson used to call them, are a distinct breed with distinct preferences. They read magazines such as the *New Yorker, Vanity Fair*, the *Economist*, and *GQ*, and the books of publishers such as Alfred A. Knopf and Farrar, Strauss and Giroux. They subscribe online or in print to newspapers such as the *New York Times* and the *Wall Street Journal*. According to those publishers' demographic profiles, their readers are a bit older, a bit richer, and a bit better educated than readers of other publications.

Their tastes are eclectic, but general educated readers are more literary-minded than data-minded, such that having science explained is not really why they read a science article. To them, a great expository scientific article or book lets them experience the subject and the people involved with it; it inspires admiration, fascination, amusement, or dismay. A good example is "Form and Fungus: Can Mushrooms Help Us Get Rid of Styrofoam?" by longtime *New Yorker* staff writer Ian Frazier, in the magazine's May 20, 2013, issue.

In a work about science's influences or implications, gerries want a firm point of view, and their interest tilts toward the cultural, societal, and political. They expect sophisticated argument regarding implications and conciseness in the science supporting the argument. Whatever the perspective, they respond to clarity, original expression, metaphor and analogy, supple language, skillful pacing, and persuasive reasoning. Thus, whether your subject is dramatic in its own right or tied to a specific question of importance, these readers will be interested, but their engagement will be proportional to the writerly care you give it.

OPINION LEADERS

Another reader whom scientists sometimes visualize is what publishers call "influentials," a category that includes leaders in government and business. But this group is fuzzy, because "opinion leader" is a marketing concept, not a reading or writing one, and a lot of academic (business-school) ink has been spilled trying to define them and their reading habits. The picture gleaned from these efforts to define them is that prominent people read what other people do, just more of it. If the readers you hope to excite are science funders or government policy makers, you can find them reading magazines such as the *New Yorker,* the *Economist, Scientific American,* and *Bloomberg Businessweek,* all of which claim that a quarter to a third of their readers are science, business, and government influentials.

However, marketing research clearly suggests that when it comes to delivering a message to influentials, the best vehicle is a newspaper. Opinion leaders apparently read more of them and spend more time on them than do newspaper readers as a whole. Ideas differ about which sections are popular with which readers, but newspaper editors agree that, after the front page, the editorial and opinion pages are the most read by all readers, print and online. The best aspect of people reading an op-ed (named for its location opposite the editorial page, not for being an opinion piece) is how engaged they are likely to be: they are reading to inform their point of view. Newspapers' and some magazines' op-ed columns are open to outside contributors, and this is an instance when being an expert rather than a professional writer is a huge advantage. The difficulty in writing op-eds lies in the form. The average length is usually fewer than a thousand words, which means giving only the most salient facts and requiring the information both to serve an argument and to be new and important. Still, for essays meeting these criteria, op-eds are great platforms.

HEALTH READERS

Health is a major interest of readers in developed countries worldwide. An example: in 2009, Rodale, the publisher of magazines such as *Prevention*, *Women's Health*, and *Running Times*, reported that global readership for *Men's Health* had passed twenty-two million. Between that report and 2012, Rodale went on to launch *Runner's World* in China, *Men's Health* in Bulgaria and Hungary, and *Women's Health* in Thailand and Germany. *Prevention* has nearly nine million readers in the United States, as well as ten international editions.

In the United States, readers of health publications are mostly in their forties and fifties, with incomes above the national average, and are slightly better educated than readers of other publications. Readers skew younger—in the early to mid-thirties—for publications in special-interest areas, such as fitness and parenting, which involve less health content but still lots of it. The important commonality among health readers is a self-oriented perspective. For example, a reader of *Men's Health* or *Women's Health* is interested in health issues that come up more often with people of his or her own sex, and someone subscribing to a fitness publication expects to find health subjects relating to fitness. The corollary is that a little science goes a long way for these readers. They realize that the biology of a disorder or phenomenon—the "why" of it—is important, but its manifestation and the way they should respond to it mean much more. When science sheds light on those aspects, it can be a good day for both author and reader.

You should not hesitate to write about health and the brain for reputable health websites and online health publications. The entire area of lay health has grown rapidly online. In print, health magazines and books are holding their own, despite the economic pressure that online reading has caused. The one exception is health reference books in print; they have rapidly lost readers to their own online versions and the new online references.

SELF-HELP READERS

Self-help readers are different from health readers: they seek prescriptive advice, lots of it, preferably as plans or programs they can use to solve a problem or to meet an objective of concern to them. These readers are fascinating—optimistic, independent, and insecure. If one promising plan doesn't work, they're off to try another. Oddly, quite a few of them distrust both science and medicine, whence comes the success of self-help programs invented by patients who lost faith in orthodox treatments. So, on the face of it, this does not seem like a neuroscience reader, but a few authors have managed to shape neuroscience into best-selling self-help material without distorting it. Think of Daniel Amen, Daniel Goleman, and John Ratey, whose books and websites have large self-help followings. Their secret is not in teaching the reader gold-standard brain science, but in knowing which neuroscience topics will genuinely motivate the reader to follow what are often prescriptions they have already heard or even thought of themselves.

POPULAR-SCIENCE READERS

The popular-science reader is still with us, for the evergreen reason that science reveals fascinating things. These readers simply like science, and working scientists are not the majority among them.

The three biggest popular-science magazines—*Popular Science, Discover,* and *Scientific American*—together have almost two and a half million readers online and in print, and most of these readers are better educated than average American adults are.* Nationally, about 26 percent of adults have some college or an associate's degree, and 30 percent have a bachelor's or advanced degree. But among the 1.3 million reading *Popular Science,* 67 percent have some college and 32 percent are professionals; of *Discover*'s 565,000 readers, 55 percent have some college education. *Scientific American,* with 491,000 readers, is considered popular science because not all its readers are scientists, but they are very highly educated; more than half are professionals, and 92 percent have a college or postgraduate degree.

You can get an idea of these readers' sensibilities from the different ways the three magazines handle graphics and text. Online, *Popular Science* is visually and textually in a hurry, almost chaotic; in print, it is more conventional, but its feature articles are short even though their subjects are often very deep. *Discover* brings to mind any number of *New York Times* "Science" section features, but with impressive graphics, and *Scientific American*

---

* http://www.census.gov/compendia/statab/2012/tables/12s0231.pdf

often seems different from a journal only in that it successfully bridges the gap between its highly trained scientist-writers and its nonscientist readers.

What the three biggest popular-science magazines have in common are lay-accessible accounts of new, unexpected, or transformative findings and portrayals of how scientific mountains are climbed. In all of them, authors mention the science's connection with matters of everyday life, but the connection is rarely the point; the science is. So if you ask yourself what you want most to present about your proposed subject, and the answer comes back, "It's the science," the popular-science reader is yours.

BLOG READERS

Millions of people read blogs, but who they are and what they want is unclear, because the blogosphere is kind of a digital big bang—incredibly vast and new. Academics and information-technology professionals have done some work to bring blog readers into better focus, and it suggests that, for stand-alone blogs, readers tend to be young and supportive of blogs by friends and others who share their hobbies or interests. These readers also seem to consider blogs as much a participatory activity as a reading activity, a feeling encouraged by the reader commentary that most blogs allow. The youth tilt fades, though, for blogs that have tens of thousands of readers or are hosted by online publications, organizations, and special-interest sites.

Developing an article to contribute to a blog may be an option; many (including the Dana Foundation's*) use guest bloggers. Discovering which ones do is hard, though. Google's search filter

---

* http://danapress.typepad.com/

can limit results to blog postings, but the thirty-nine million results for "brain blog" are not a huge help. The first Google page of *un*filtered results for the same term is slightly more informative, offering a handful of articles about brain blogs, such as "10 Best Brain Blogs" (a 2009 guest blog on blogs.com). One of these blogs, the well-regarded Brain Blogger, has set up submission guidelines* that might reflect what other blogs would also ask you about a proposed contribution. Since one of the settled features of blogging is that posts are short—typically fewer than 750 words (except for BrainBlogger, which does not impose a word count)—your first decision has to be whether a blog is even suitable for what (and the way) you want to write.

On the other hand, starting your own blog (or teaming up with a colleague to do it) would be a great way to tell an ongoing story about the brain, to freely roam the area you love. But a stand-alone blog is also a micropublishing enterprise. For example, you would have to be prepared to don a marketer's hat, at least temporarily, because the biggest hurdle in blogging seems to be getting the attention of readers. Another task is the familiar one of determining the reader you want and making sure posts stay attuned to that reader—something you wouldn't have an editor to remind you to do. You'd also have to decide what to do about reader commentary, since blog readers are ardent about having their say. Allowing reader input means screening for obscenities and libel as well as responding to at least some of the comments. It's worth spending some time online to consider what bloggers themselves have to say about publishing this way. They do a lot of blogging about blogging, and they share tips, including advice they've solicited from readers. Search "who are the readers for blogs."

---

* http://brainblogger.com/call/

SOCIAL NETWORKERS

Social-media demographics suggest an alluring pool of potential readers. According to the blog Pingdom, drawing on the Google Display Network Ad Planner, majorities using the most popular sites are thirty-five and older—specifically, 55 percent of Twitter users, 65 percent of Facebook users, and 79 percent of LinkedIn users. Across the spectrum of about a dozen social sites, the average age was nearly thirty-seven, and more were women than were men. Another site, Mashable.com, shows data from several sources reporting that upward of 80 percent of social-media users have some college or a bachelor's or higher degree, and 60 percent or more earn above the median income.

In a social-network frame of mind, however, users aren't reading. A Nielsen report surveyed 1,865 adults about what they do on these sites and found the main activities were personal and practical: staying in touch with family and friends, finding out about products and services, and doing career networking. Among "Lifestyle/Entertainment" uses, about half said they sought "how-to" information, and 67 percent said they used the sites for "entertainment," a category that, for some, might include keeping up with new ideas in science. Social networkers have told other researchers that social media are their primary way to get news, and they send news links to other networkers and vice versa. Thus, these would be places to create interest in what you might want to write about while planning to publish it elsewhere.

Taking advantage of social media could be fun if you're not shy. Rather than sending out links only after your work is published, you could have users "follow" and "like" you on Twitter and Facebook. Many users regularly follow people in their own field or in one related to it, or they discover someone to follow by way of a search term. For example, a user collecting information about brain cancer or autism might start following a researcher who is posting lay-language updates on progress and problems in the research or calling attention to new findings reported at professional meetings. A user's decision to follow or to like is influenced by both the poster's personality and the follower's interest in the subject or the authority. You can't know how this might work out for you until you are in the middle of it and getting feedback.

Feedback is what makes social media social. Users expect to have a role—to participate, to talk, and to share interests. This virtual community is a lot like a physical one. According to a study reported in the May 2012 *Harvard Business Review*, whiners aren't welcome; a sense of humor is. Self-promotion works, and so does consulting followers. And, as the volume of news clips and links passed among users attests, new information is valued. What seals the deal, though, is recognizing the community—for example, all followers receiving your reply to one follower's interesting comment, when the reply is worded in a way that also shares the comment. Users' ability to get into and remain in the action is why social media are so popular.

Many good writers use social media, but writing well is not a prerequisite. To the contrary, standards are so low as to be nonexistent. Nobody starts following anybody else in admiration of his or her grammar or spelling (especially not their spelling), but nobody stops because someone writes too well, either. According to a 2012 Mashable.com feature about the top authors on Twitter, William Shakespeare had 6,771 tweets and 23,337 followers. All is not lost.

BOOKWORMS

While publishers don't have a good demographic game, people who like books also like talking about them, and book lovers' comments on the Internet often include something about themselves, which can be enlightening. You know about Amazon.com's reader reviews, but there are more interesting and personal reader comments on Goodreads.com, a five-million-plus-member virtual book club (which Amazon bought in early 2013 but promised to leave independent). Type in the name of a lay book about the brain by a neuroscientist—a book that you admire and assume is popular—and see why readers did or didn't like it. If the project you have in mind is a book, and you think you know how you're going to write it, Goodreads might give you a good feel for who will be reading it.

As you think about these readers and decide which ones will like what you plan to write, remember that general readers are drawn to reading what they can talk about, use, or find stimulating and rewarding. Writing for them will be different from teaching, writing for journals, contributing to textbooks, and lecturing at meetings. In those settings, your ability to go into whatever detail it takes to show that your information is airtight is a mark of excellence, one you worked hard to attain. That's how you may feel the "curse": forgoing rigor and comprehensiveness to make your subject interesting and absorbing for less demanding people. You might even start wondering what it's worth if your reader doesn't need to replicate what you discuss and has no career riding on it. But touching the lay reader is a skill, too—an excellence in itself, as well as a contribution to the public good and a credit to your field. For that reason, the pursuit you've undertaken really is worthwhile.

4
YOUR VOICE

SOME writers think of voice as style, but the two terms are different. Voice is the sense of the person behind the writing. It's not as clear as Mom's voice on the phone, but, like a physical one, a writing voice is unique to the writer, and it is a flexible instrument of expression. With your writing, as with pitch, you can dial it up or dial it down and add a chuckle or a sneer, a whisper or a shout. Your voice reveals your tendency toward dialogue or monologue, toward sociability, storytelling, rumination, exploration, or thoroughness. You can consciously take advantage of any of these qualities in yourself or consciously constrain them, and to the extent that you see their effect on your narrative, you do both.

In short, your writing voice combines your technical style—syntax, grammar, and usage—and the influence of your personality on your writing. On the "listening" side of the conversation, the reader is interested in what's on the writer's mind and wants to appreciate the thinking behind the writing and adjust to it—and the reader gathers much of that insight from the writer's voice.

The way I want to talk about this is to pigeonhole a few scientific voices, try to show why readers like those voices, and explain how sometimes a writer messes up his or her voice. The caveat is that these are inventions, stereotypes. Everybody has a little of every voice, and that's why a writer might be able to write about scientific findings or issues or histories or dramas. But, like the timbre of a physical voice, the way a writer thinks tends to persist across subjects.

THE ENTHUSIAST

In writing, the enthusiast flat-out adores the science; he or she can no more refrain from loving detail than fly to the moon. Talking about it is a joy, and listening, if you can keep up with the information, is also a joy, because ardor is infectious. This is also an insistent voice, and the wise enthusiast, knowing that voice can overwhelm, uses imaginative vocabulary to describe the abstruse and makes associations with nonscientific objects, events, and dynamics. When he or she senses that the reader will fall behind despite these techniques, the enthusiast wraps it up and moves on to the next point.

It doesn't always work that way. The text will have started with the kind of rush the enthusiast can give—anecdotal or cinematic or universal in appeal and promising, "You'll love what comes next." And the reader, spotting the formidable intelligence behind the words and feeling smarter by the minute, will have fallen for it. (Remember, "makes me smarter" is a key value of leisure readers.) The writer was great company—until the voice changed.

When an enthusiast's voice grows hoarse, the sound of lecturing creeps in, as if, instead of keeping his or her elbows on table, decanter between "us," the writer has stepped away and mounted the podium. It is the sound of detail morphing into tutorial, the sight of instructional phrases peppering the text: "we shall see," "as we have seen," "as mentioned above, we now must . . . ," or "next, we will see . . ." Worst, perhaps, is the phrase "those of you," or a similar locution that reveals the writer is addressing readers in multiples when reading is a one-on-one experience.

The thing is, this is not the natural mien of the enthusiast; this writer would be mortified to see someone wriggling in his or her chair or looking around to see who else was implicated in "those of you." All that's happened is that the enthusiast has wearied—did I mention writing is hard?—and, determined not to give in to fatigue, is tiring the reader, too.

THE AMIABLE VOICE

The writing of the amiable scientist is easygoing while telling a serious story, conversational in both formal and informal contexts, and occasionally opinionated. Personal references and anecdotes come easily. Technical explanation is often quick and specific, and more detailed exposition is clear, compact, and unadorned. The opposite of insistent, the amiable voice can be so relaxed as to give the reader an impulse to speak up.

Offering the reader intellectual equality, as this voice does, is disarming; it makes the reader feel like a participant in the scientific work or debate the writer is describing. The companionability has great appeal to the reader who looks to reading as "my reward for doing other things." A reader motivated by "makes me smarter" might prefer to be challenged more aggressively but still reads with interest when the writer's credentials are good, as he or she knows the smarts are there to be had.

Do you have an amiable writing voice? Does it get weary? Go hoarse? How might you lose it? Why am I asking all these questions? That's what the amiable voice does when it falters:

asks questions. Relaxed writers sometimes get so comfortable with the reader that their internal debate about what to say next turns into part of the text. I've seen as many as six questions open a new topic by a writer who, until then, had been in charge of the narrative—as if the writer were about to cry out, "I'm lost!" That's the benign impression.

Less benign is the impression that the writer is demanding we pay attention (maybe there will be a quiz at the end). Questions that give this impression aren't the same as rhetorical questions—which we like, because we know the answers—and they're not anticipating our own questions, a strategy that, when used sparingly, can be good writing. They're questions created to start new information, and the problem is that they prompt us to hunt mentally for answers we're not equipped to give.

THE COMPREHENSIVE WRITER

The comprehensive writing voice tends to be low-key, judiciously inflected, and good with the big picture as well as the pixels in it. The comprehensive writing voice seems to come from policy-related situations, and when in good form it has just enough gravitas and is even toned, well-spoken, thorough, and imbued with a sense of the engaged person behind it. Often, a comprehensive science-writing voice is a voice from professional-interest leadership, and a person who adopts this voice is a very good writer of newspaper op-eds and where-things-stand kinds of magazine articles.

Readers easily recognize the comprehensive voice, and those who gravitate to it like the feeling that the comprehensive writer can, and intends to, concisely answer decisive lay questions about a subject. They're in a subcategory of the "makes me smarter" mode: they're reading with a desire to be well informed about a specific subject, and comprehensive writing rarely disappoints. But when it does . . .

Overpacked is the word for the comprehensive voice gone awry. Any writer can be intense, and when a comprehensive lets go, he or she doesn't expostulate. Instead, the case for the premise gets made in too many ways or marshals too many details. The tip-off is a sentence growing to fifty or more words, able to give an English teacher diagramming nightmares. That's a comprehensive in a frenzy.

THE INTELLECTUAL VOICE

By *intellectual* I mean people who like learning for its own sake, people whose second nature is to immerse themselves in subjects they're interested in. The best intellectual writing voices seem to combine depth of learning with felicity of expression and empathy, along with the writer's taste for high-level subjects. The use of vocabulary is pleasing—rich and appropriate—and lay associations with well-known facts and ideas are graceful. The voice is one that never seems to talk down.

Lay readers looking to "reward myself" join the "makes me smarter" set in gravitating to this voice that promises much and delivers generously. The reward comes as much from pleasure in the voice itself as it comes from the differentness of the subject, and the smarts a reader may gain are a given.

Predictably, if the intellectual voice goes off pitch, it's not with scientific jargon but with ten-dollar words and obscure references or concepts. The writer has not so much deserted readers as forgotten them; blissed out in the warm sea of knowledge, he or she doesn't notice readers drowning.

THE THEORIST

The theorist's voice is creative. He or she likes making connections and thinking of reasons for things that no one else has thought of. It is a friendly, accommodating voice with an expectant tone, nudging readers to "think outside the box" along with the writer.

Depending on the theorist's attitude toward well-established facts, smarts- and reward-seeking readers are on board, especially for fresh takes on well-worn subjects. A different reader also engages with the theorist: the one who likes to be able to "talk about and share" or who finds the perspective "utilitarian." Health and self-help readers recognize the voice, and they like it.

The theorist's voice needs to be well managed from the outset, because a good scientist writing creatively about science is on a tightrope: a too-cautious tone separating evidence from speculation makes "utilitarian" and "talk-and-share" readers uncertain, and a brash or hypey tone makes "reward" and "smarts" readers skeptical.

The important thing about voice is that it allows the reader to see who you are in your writing. Even as you adjust it for "conversation" with a lay reader and talk about your science differently from the way you talk about it with colleagues, you'll still be you—the same person writing as when not writing. That's what makes it so important to flush out the perspective that gave you the idea of writing for a lay reader. As you can tell, your work is likely to fall comfortably into one of the many kinds of reading people like, and you can be sure it will fit one of the many reasons people like to read. But you also can be sure the experience will be a struggle if you don't discern your alignment with a lay reader, because your default will be to your peers—and that will bring on the "curse of knowledge" full-blown.

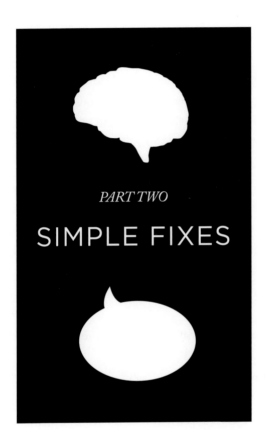

PART TWO

SIMPLE FIXES

INTRODUCTION

TRUE STORY: One summer Friday a few years ago, an
editor at a general-interest publishing house called me. Months
earlier, his firm and our foundation had agreed to copublish
several books. Now he had one of the manuscripts and was
trying to read it, but, he said, "I keep putting it down."
My thought was, "Hah, more science than he can handle," but
I also had received a copy, so I promised to read it over the
weekend and suggested we talk the following week. Then I called
a friend who had received a copy, too, and asked if he had read it.

"It's soporific," he said gloomily. "I'm not sure what to suggest."

"You'll figure it out," I said, making a note to look up *soporific*.

I found out what it meant the next day, but not from the
dictionary. After settling on my sunny porch to read the
manuscript, I soon dozed off. When I woke, I blamed the
warm weather and decided to do a little copy editing to stay
awake—to banish the cobwebs by getting hands-on. Only a few
pages into it, I saw that it hadn't been the heat that had put me
to sleep. The manuscript had. So many of its sentences began,
"There is," "There are," "It is," "It was"—ticktock, ticktock, like a
metronome. It was hypnosis by pronoun.

Hardly anything is more dismaying than hearing that your writing doesn't engage the reader and not knowing why. You thought you did such a good job. The subject is inherently interesting, and you are an authority on it. You had a fascinating perspective, presented good information, made the science understandable, and avoided jargon. You lavished attention on the reader's stake. You even included some jokes. Yet, you're told, your editors didn't finish it; somehow, they had to put it down.

Of course, your piece could need an overhaul—refocusing, reorganizing, adding text, deleting passages. But hold that thought for now. The problem can easily come from everyday words and phrases used carelessly or repetitively such that they produce a kind of torpor or vagueness in the narrative. Much of this type of wording is imported from speech, where it serves a purpose: to slow the flow of substance and to give a listener time to digest what's being said. My guess is that a listening brain needs this, perhaps also to process the speaker's facial expressions, gestures, and so on, and to organize a physical response as well as a mental one. When we are reading, however, the same words and phrases are superfluous, and that's why the boredom creeps in. These little fillers are small in number, but fixing them can make a big difference.

5

SOPORIFICS

A mere handful of particular expressions can make a narrative boring enough to put you to sleep. They do this by slowing the writing, making it humdrum, or producing creeping difficulty in paying attention. Vetting your writing to fix soporifics is a good way to energize and sharpen text. Better yet, if you can make yourself avoid them in the first place, the writing will be more rewarding, because what tires or bores a reader often has the same effect on the drafting writer.

There is/are

Of all the dreary usages, starting sentences with *There is/are* must top the list. Nearly always, the phrase means nothing. All the words with shape, weight, sound, texture, or energy are downstream from it. Even worse, among the waiting words are the sentence's real subject and verb, weakened by demotion to second place. Since *There is/are* slows the momentum of a narrative and softens the concrete of a sentence, using it repetitively drains the life from a manuscript. Look at the lift a sentence gets from removing *There are*:

> There are now hundreds of scientists investigating sports-related brain injuries.

Now, hundreds of scientists are investigating sports-
related brain injuries.

The soft fuzz of *There is/are* has a few good uses. It can help
ease the narrative pace or clearly separate two thoughts. For
example, starting a sentence with "There is . . ." can separate
two complex ideas that will make a sentence too hard for
a lay reader to digest if they are joined with a conjunction.
Such an overly complex sentence might be, for example:

> In clinical studies of DBS for treatment-resistant
> depression, investigators implant the electrodes in
> a region that is hyperactive in depressed patients,
> Brodmann Area 25, because this region connects not
> only with the hypothalamus, the regulator of basics such
> as sleep and appetite, but also with three other structures
> disturbed in depression.

The better form would be:

> In clinical studies of DBS for treatment-resistant
> depression, investigators implant the electrodes in
> a region that is hyperactive in depressed patients,
> Brodmann Area 25. There is a good reason for using
> Area 25: it connects not only with the hypothalamus,
> a regulator of basic activities such as sleep and
> appetite, but also with three other structures
> disturbed in depression.

There is/are is also useful for prioritizing, slightly
downplaying the sentence it starts. This softening might be

necessary to keep the reader clear on which of two adjacent points is more important or might be desirable to keep the direction of the story clear. It is useful, for example, when the sentence serves only to add texture, as in the following passage:

> The leaders of the study had reported to Smith that they believed it should be stopped. There was the expected grumbling among the postdocs, but they saw the problem, too. Smith made the decision soon after reviewing the group's data.

There is/are can be preferable when what follows would be stilted or would have to be said in a way that is unsuited to the rest of the text. For example, consider "There is no reason to think . . .": You could change that to "No reason exists to think . . ." but it would seem stilted. You could avoid *There is* if you've been addressing the reader as "you"—just make it "You should not think . . ." But if you have been writing more formally, you're in luck with *There is*, because here it actually does its job as a pronoun, politely standing in for You.

Finally, *There is/are* can help you avoid unintended implications. For example, you've described a new scientific consensus and want to mention the old consensus without seeming to disparage anyone who still holds to it. "There is still some belief that . . ." is better than a snarky "Some scientists still believe . . ."

Bottom line: banishing *There is/are* from your writing would be silly. What's important is to remember its pronounced weakening effect and to use it purposefully.

It is/was . . . that

It is/was is a paradox: a heads-up phrase in a tiny package. And, as with *There is/was*, overusing it exacts a price in reader attention. Compare these two uses:

> *It is obvious that . . .* (the "heads-up" usage; more formal than "obviously" would be)

> *It is the thinking of most scientists that . . .* (dull; it should be "Most scientists think . . .")

Most of the time, the *It is/was . . . that* construct is just dull. And, sometimes, it can actually confuse the reader. One such instance is when a writer begins a sentence with "It is" or "It was" right after a series, such as a recitation of brain features or ideas about the brain. Intending only to pause before moving on to discuss one item from the series, the author writes, for example, "It was [the item] that seemed to explain most of the issues, so they planned the next steps on that basis. . ." The trouble is that this infinitesimal pause, the heads-up before we learn what you're about to say, is a form of suspense. It prompts us to get ready for the extra significance that "It was" implies, and when the next point seems no weightier than those preceding it, the reader gets a feeling that he or she may have failed to grasp something important.

In that example, the item is singled out only to continue a discussion, and "It was" is superfluous. However, if the item that has been singled out marks the end of one topic and the start of another in the narrative, the heads-up is valuable: "It was [the item] that, today, seems most likely to yield the first effective drug. Based on that finding, the focus now is on . . ."

Whether it is used to be forceful or to add a slight flourish, *It is/was* is worth preserving for the purpose of alerting the reader to pay attention to what comes next. If the phrase appears too often for no particular reason, not only does our interest flag, but also we become desensitized to it. It loses its ability to get our attention and leaves you, the writer, looking for less quick and nimble ways to do so.

a number of

Microsoft Word's thesaurus lists eleven synonyms for *a number of.* They range from *none* to *countless*—showing how meaningless the phrase is. It is another migrant from conversation: someone asks, "Why?" and we shrug and say, "Oh, *a number of* reasons." The unspoken message is, "It's not worth spelling out."

The logic for using *a number of* in writing is different. The writer has a magnitude in mind, uses *a number of* to signify it, and depends on context to suggest which of the eleven possible synonyms it might mean. Though the phrase is both lazy and boring, it works well enough for common subjects about which—from personal experience or news exposure—the reader can guess what magnitude the phrase represents.

In writing about the brain for lay readers, however, failing to be more specific hurts the text more than it would if you were writing about, say, class-action lawsuits. Lay readers are less likely to have a feel for what *a number of* means in research and, finding it unclear, are more likely to interpret it as the conversational signal: "this line of discussion is not worth pursuing." Therefore, besides being meaningless, *a number of* can euthanize the fact tied to it. At a minimum, signifiers of number (such as *many, several, dozens, a multitude,* and *a few*) or proportion (such as *most, a majority,* or *nearly all*) are better because they are clearer. But when the point involved is fairly important to an immediate scientific discussion, it may also be desirable to add some context. If space allows, a construct such as "In the past decade, ...dozens of studies have looked at [topic] and most found that ..." may do more to sharpen the point in the reader's mind.

in fact and *indeed*

In fact and *indeed* are intensifiers, very handy in conversation and in pedagogy—sort of like tour guides' bright hats, signaling the leaders of a crowd. *Indeed* is the more versatile of the two. With the right tone of voice or facial expression, it can signify "I kid you not" or "I don't believe it"; it can be stern, as in "You will *indeed* do it," or sarcastic, as in "*Indeed*, it was the only thing you did." *In fact* has only one job: to introduce the clincher convincing listeners that something they just heard is really, really true.

Neither phrase has the same effect in writing; rather, both are flat. They are superfluous because the reasons for using them in speech are not (or should not be) present. As readers, we put ourselves in your hands with the assumption that you would not kid us or scold us or need to reassure us that what you just wrote is true. Since these reasons should not be necessary, they create uncertainty about or even diminish the very points they are used to intensify.

You may wonder what to do about a fact you've left in

suspense or suspect the reader may doubt. Better than *in fact* or *indeed* is to refer specifically to the fact's final disposition. Instead of "*Indeed,* the transmitter proved to be inhibitory," consider "More studies were necessary, but finally it was clear that . . ." If the point needs clinching, try this: "Evidence grew, until Smith's study erased all doubt . . ."

In my experience, *in fact* and *indeed* show up when a writer is becoming fatigued after a long day of writing. My advice would be: if you feel one of these expressions coming on, take note, close the file for the day, and go back to it tomorrow. Refreshed, you will surely find a better way of saying it.

complex (and its variations)

If you serve your friends an exotic dish, do you pass it to them saying, "It has ingredients you're not used to; you may not like it"? Probably not. More likely, you share your pleasure at introducing them to it, and maybe you tell them about the first time you tried it. So why do so many scientists cue up essential information for general readers as if they may not be able to handle it?

Too often, the opening sentence of an explanation goes like this: "The [disease/phenomenon] is highly complex," "Complex rules are built into the [neural feature]," "The complexities are numerous," or "The [phenomenon] is one of the most complicated functions of the brain."

Pointing to complexity is common in journals, so my guess is that these constructs are a feature of writing for peers, who must need to consider complexity in research. The general reader, on the other hand, has no need to be warned of complexity in an explanation or discussion.

Starting off that way makes us wary that you are about to tell us more than we need to know—and you're going to confuse us in the process. That prophecy can be self-fulfilling. Sadder yet, if you have done your job and written the information to be perfectly clear to someone untrained, setting off alarm bells means shooting yourself in the foot.

The best use of *complex* and its variations is when complexity is important in itself. One instance is in writing about disorders that refuse to yield useful answers, such as autism and Alzheimer's disease, when the reader is hoping you will say a cure is around the corner. Mentioning how complex the science is can help us be realistic as readers, but the challenge is to say it in a way that encourages us to keep reading—in a way that makes it clear you are bringing up complexity as a research issue, not warning that your discussion will be hard to follow.

Describing or commenting on complexity as a challenge of research enhances some kinds of texts. It can make for the kind of good storytelling that general readers, and especially popular-science readers, enjoy. In articles and in books whose length allows you to share a sense of the scientist's life in addition to presenting the science, such nuances are interesting and add to the reader's appreciation of the science.

Bottom line: if you still feel a need to introduce a discussion by referring to its complexity, take another look at how you have written, or plan to write, the discussion. It probably could be made simpler and clearer.

It might seem odd that the few common words and phrases targeted in this chapter would be pernicious. In writing about a familiar subject, they are probably less so (though they are still unimaginative). When it comes to well-known topics, people have plenty of existing knowledge and opinions; thus, even if the writing is flat, they can engage with the ideas anyway. The reader interested in a brain question is less sure and less quick to see what you're saying. In effect, your writing is held to a higher standard.

6
TAMING THE UNDERBRUSH

WE expect novelists to stew over language—it's how they make the imaginary real—but we don't picture writers of articles and nonfiction books doing that. We suppose the facts are the thing, and any fussing would involve selecting and organizing them in an interesting way. If we admire or dislike nonfiction we read, we think of the overall impression it made: boring or riveting, lyrical or plodding, humorous or touching, mean or generous, and so on. Those impressions are mash-ups of the author's language, style, and voice, but language is at the root of all. Good nonfiction writers pay intense attention to language. Style and voice don't lend themselves to revision; they are mostly settled at the outset, the results of a writer's decisions about the subject, the perspective, and the reader. Language, on the other hand, can either successfully execute what you're trying to say or kill you—and poor language choices add up to death by a thousand cuts.

In science manuscripts, certain usages tend to inflict these cuts. When they proliferate, they fill a manuscript with uncertainty. The three I'll discuss in this chapter—jargon, passive voice, and negative wording—can make passages complicated and dense. They are like underbrush clogging an untended walking trail. You've heard warnings against the first two a thousand times, so my focus is on convincing you to heed them. The third, negative wording, is commonplace, neither good nor bad, but using it thoughtlessly in science-related material takes a toll.

JARGON

Before writing for or speaking to a lay audience, scientists are almost always told, "Don't use jargon!" Few people explain exactly why this is important, and when reading a manuscript I often get the feeling that the author is skeptical about this advice. This is especially true when I read longer manuscripts, in which the author starts off solicitous of the lay reader, but then terminology begins piling up.

Let me offer what I believe is the best argument for seeing jargon as hazardous material: the reader will stop reading. Recall the Northwestern University research into the reasons that lay readers engage with their reading: "talk about and share," "makes me smarter," "my reward for doing other things." In an article or book about the brain, the reader's ability to derive these rewards depends on the clarity of technical information. When readers realize they are struggling with terminology, the reward goes out of the effort. Deflation even affects readers who might be expected to try harder—for instance, those reading about a disorder that involves them. But these readers may actually give up more easily, because talking about or passing on what they've read is not a reward but a need.

Dumping jargon is hard, because language you use every day doesn't seem like jargon, and you may harbor a wish that everyone would want to learn more of it. But whatever lay readers may need or want to recall, they have to do it in their own language. Most have no reason to use scientific terms in their social or work lives, and verbiage not used is verbiage that doesn't stick.

You might be thinking, "Hold on. If this were true, how did *neuron* and *synapse* make it into the vernacular? These words even appear in TV scripts and in stand-up comedy. They weren't there twenty years ago." The smart-aleck answer is, advertising. The right answer, though, is that *you* made them relevant—via your research and, subsequently, via people writing about your research in multiple contexts, including pharmaceutical ad copy. It also helps that these words are short, easy to pronounce, and easily illustrated with simple drawings.

You face a dilemma when it seems you must use scientific language at some point. Some important brain terms are barely pronounceable—think *oligodendrocyte*—much less dulcet enough to capture a lay person's fancy. And with *posterior medial temporal gyrus*, you know you're headed deep into "Huh?" territory.

You can solve this dilemma by asking yourself why you think you need to use the scientific name in question. If it seems necessary because it's part of how you understand the brain and you want to be thorough, that's reason enough if it is in your author/reader compact. That is, when your reader has every expectation that you will go into technical detail, such as in a popular-science article or in a disorder-centered article plainly offered as "the science behind X." It's also appropriate to use the scientific term if you are clearly writing from a personal perspective, such as in a memoir about an important discovery. The reader knows the context is deeply technical and expects to encounter some daunting terminology. (In this case, however, know when enough is enough. The reader is interested in what it's like to be you or to be there, not in knowing everything you know.)

In most other writing for lay readers, the same thoroughness will crowd out the perspective that you chose and that the reader expects. Thus, the best way to tame your jargon is to remember *why* you are writing what you are writing. The jargon dilemma usually rears its head when you lose sight of your objective, and if you do, the reader does, too. You both get lost in the woods. Hence, most of the time the solution is simple and brutal: eliminate the jargon, *and* eliminate whatever you are using it to say.

When you can't avoid jargon—you may need *oligodendrocyte* to write about multiple sclerosis, for example—make it interesting, because doing so gives your reader a way to notice and remember it. For instance note that the word sounds a little like *oleomargarine*; make it welcome so that it is a good companion to yet another word you'll have to use, *myelin*. The reader will recognize that the attention you are paying to a word as a word means that it is important to digest and remember.

It isn't necessary to play up an unavoidable technical word that you have good reason to think your reader has been exposed to. For example, *hippocampus* has been making the rounds in most writing about memory and aging, as well as PTSD. Still, as a courtesy to the reader and to be on the safe side, this is a good example of when to accentuate a word in parentheses—e.g., "... *hippocampus* (from the Greek for "seahorse," which it resembles) ..."

Finally, most of the time, if a necessary passage could become thick with jargon, the best solution is to focus on what it adds up to and to compose a fully lay-worded rendition of the point. The worst solution is to use the technical terms followed by lay translations in parentheses. Besides being unimaginative and making a passage hard to follow, the parentheses turn into a kind of visual jargon, making the text look even more complicated than it is.

PASSIVE VOICE

The big rap on the passive voice is that, most of the time, it is poor writing. In a passive-voice sentence, the cart is before the horse: the actor is secondary or unmentioned, and the object of the action is in the position of the sentence's subject. The criticism is that putting actor after action saps energy from the action and makes it harder to visualize. For example, "The door to the murder room was quickly opened for them by the cop guarding it." To see the action, the reader mentally flips the sentence: "The cop guarding the door to the murder room quickly opened it for them." What makes the passive voice tedious is that a reader is already supplying detail to the picture—the cop's arms and legs, blue uniform, cap, walkie-talkie, gun—so the extra chore of putting actor and action in order is a nuisance.

In ordinary reading, at least the content is recognizable. In a scientific discussion, the passive can be a double hit, because the content is unfamiliar. The reader is usually working hard to retain previous detail from the text—detail certainly not as rich or three-dimensional to the reader as it is to the writer—making it all the harder for the reader to mentally flip an action from passive to active and be confident of understanding it.

Scientists have told me that the passive voice is a habit because it has been a rule in journal writing forever, as a mark of rectitude taking the focus off who did research and putting it on what was done. It's easy to think that similar use of the passive should be fine with the lay reader when you are explaining science and the reader knows that's what you are doing. But the lay reader is a leisure reader taking a break (or a needy one trying to deal with a disorder), not a colleague digesting a study. Painting the picture in vigorous active-voice sentences can make the difference between engagement and disengagement.

Even in text where the content is ordinary—"three papers about the finding were presented," for example—the passive calls for the lay reader to conjure up the setting, the person who did the presenting, and the manner of presentation. This is all obvious to the scientist writing it, but not necessarily to the reader. In this case, the straightforwardness of the active voice helps the writer: it is easier to see when you are leaving out information that the reader may not be able to supply. It forces you to provide context, or to remain within one you've provided, and makes it clearer when you are heading into unnecessary territory. In other words, it helps keep both you and the reader out of the underbrush.

Having said all this, the passive exists for a good reason: often the object of an action belongs ahead of the subject and verb, because the object is the thing you are writing about, and using the active voice will shift attention to a secondary actor. But even then, it depends on the picture you are trying to draw. Here's a simple example—a dog story:

> The dog headed for the open door. He was followed by the cat.

> The dog headed for the open door. The cat followed him.

Both passages are fine, but each gives a slightly different impression. In the first, the passive voice suggests a story about how the dog got out and took the cat with him. In the second, the active voice suggests a hapless dog being stalked by a cat—that is, it's a two-actor situation, and the cat gets active-voice standing along with the dog.

NEGATIVE WORDING

By "negative wording" I mean the popular construct that goes, "This is not X, but rather Y." The usage tells the reader, "Wait. It's not what you might think."

The classic purpose of negative wording is to keep the reader clear about a narrative's meaning and direction. This snippet from a *Wall Street Journal* book review is a good example: "The train-based travel book is of course a popular subgenre—think of Paul Theroux. Yet 'Italian Ways' isn't, in the author's words, 'exactly a travel book.'" The reviewer knows that, based on how he's described the book so far, the reader is thinking it is like other travel books. He uses the negative construct both to correct a probable misconception and to heighten interest in what's different about the book.

But such careful usage is rare. The negative construct is becoming a device. It is almost typical of writing for highly educated readers, sometimes merely to vary sentence structure or, often, to display the writer's knowledge of an object or idea even if the reader is not likely to be envisioning the thing the writer is dismissing. Some skillful writers also have found that the construct adds a touch of languor to their style, because a time-out for contemplating what a subject *isn't* de-energizes a text; the mini-digression uses up some of the forward momentum of the main ideas in the narrative.

But, in science writing, indiscriminate mention of things or ideas only to wave the reader away from them weakens the reader's understanding. It puts too much emphasis on what something is *not* and too little on making sure the reader knows what it *is*, especially if a writer gets caught up discussing a point in terms of what it's not. When the reader doesn't know much about either X or Y, it's just a bad idea.

Sometimes, though, you can feel compelled to tell the reader that what you are saying is not what the reader might think. At those times you are most likely writing a lay narrative about one of many popular brain-related topics—for example, the aging brain. You know your reader may have preconceptions and misconceptions from other reading, and you are anxious to set your information apart from low-quality ideas "out there." So you reach for "Y is not X."

Try not to. For some subjects, you could wind up loading your manuscript with denials, and the reader will think, "If it's not this and not that, what the heck is it?" Or, worse, if the misinformation is livelier and easier to digest than the facts you are explaining, your reader may see your dismissal of the misinformation as defensive, just a way to justify making him miserable with something overly complicated. You'll have denied your way into the underbrush.

The first line of defense is to put the irrelevant or erroneous information out of your mind and put your heart into making your own information interesting and convincing. Sell it. Arm your reader to be the know-it-all with friends and family by regaling them with the news you are giving them. If you write like you mean it, the chances are good you won't even need to mention whatever you do not want the reader thinking of.

By not wasting the reader's focus on unnecessary negative constructs, a writer preserves them for when nothing else will do. That is to say, some wrong ideas become so popular that they can cause a reader to misunderstand or even discount what you are writing. That's when a negative construct can be strong and effective. For example, "Video games are not inherently able to boost cognition. Rather, research is beginning to find that some kinds of specially designed games can be used with training to improve memory and attention in the elderly."

In short, avoid the stylish negative in favor of writing so that the reader, who is carefully attending to your words, stays fully absorbed in the information you are providing.

7
MAKING IT CLEAR

THIS chapter deals with words that create problems with clarity when the context is scientific. They comprise a very small subset of ordinary English words that are best to use sparingly or to avoid. They have an outsize effect in a science-related text for the reason provided in the previous chapter: the reader's unfamiliarity with the subject.

But these words come with a difference. They also can trip up an editor, especially a generalist editor; they have a way of sailing right past us. We don't know we've mistaken their meaning; all we know is that something isn't very clear. The upshot is, we start making editing suggestions that don't solve the problem and might even make it worse. Often, a copy editor will flag these words at the last minute, but far better is to resist them while writing, when you can come up with either a synonym or good prose to express the idea.

These troublesome words are crossover words, unblessed usages, and pronouns.

CROSSOVER WORDS

These are everyday words that have become important in neuroscience. Scientists recognize what they mean, and they may use them in their writing in a way that is clear to a lay reader, too. But when the usage is unclear, readers get lost or misled. Crossovers are especially common causes of this problem.

Function (in all its forms). *Function* is both a noun and a verb, and it also has adjective, adverb, and gerund forms. It is regularly the most overused—and, to me, the most unwelcome—word in any neuroscience manuscript. Its meaning is totally context dependent, both in everyday use (where it has three definitions and can have some two dozen specific meanings) and in neuroscience, where it can refer to anything from a neural purpose, role, or task to performing, operating, or behaving.

The following is typical of the way *function* turns up in neuroscience manuscripts:

> The temporal lobes have important functions and are concerned with hearing and visual function.

This seems to say the lobes have important roles, but it is ambiguous as to whether they have a major responsibility or facilitate other brain operations, thus making it hard to tell if the rest says that the lobes affect how hearing and vision operate or just exchange information with them. A lay reader who is only beginning to get a fix on brain geography and circuits can't possibly guess what the sentence means.

Ideally, you would never use *function* at all. Instead you would use unambiguous synonyms, such as *role*, *job*, *operates*, or *works*. A defensible exception is when a description immediately before or after *function* makes its meaning clear—for example, "The hippocampus sends information to long-term memory, and PTSD impairs this function" (though better writing would provide PTSD's specific effect, from which we could infer "impairs this function").

Mediate. For you, it is clear when *mediate* means "to drive a phenomenon" (as in, "Adaptive habits are mediated by the release of dopamine into the prefrontal cortex and the striatum") or "to be responsible for a faculty" (as in, "A key component of those neural circuits in the prefrontal cortex that mediate working memory is the pyramidal neuron"). But the *mediate* that most people know—"to resolve or settle disputes by working with the conflicting parties"—is constantly reinforced in everyday life. Thus, the ordinary meaning of *mediate* controls what the reader perceives and makes the biological mechanism or process seem like a kind of ball bearing—as if its job is only to smooth out the interaction between more important mechanisms. In many manuscripts, the use of *mediate* is a case of slipping into jargon and is easy to fix; the writer can simply substitute the plain verb that says what's going on. In some manuscripts, however, *mediate* marks a narrative becoming unnecessarily complex, digressing far from the perspective the writer began with, and the solution is the same as when any other jargon begins to thicken: backtrack with the delete key, all the way to where you went off track.

Modulate. As with *mediate*, the lay and neuroscience meanings of *modulate* are different, and the lay meaning is too ingrained for a reader to hesitate when seeing the word. The lay definition—"to tune a sound or a frequency to a key or pitch," or, for example, "to balance speakers on an audio system"—has, in effect, narrowed lay understanding to volume control. Thus, sentences such as "Visual signals are modulated by the behavioral state and needs of the animal" or "The vocalizations of one monkey modulate the brain processes going on in the other monkey" seem to say that modulators merely raise or lower the intensity of the thing modulated. Any more interactive, subtle, or multidimensional relationship between them is lost for the lay reader, so that whatever follows is all the fuzzier. Unlike *mediate*, which usually has a lay synonym, *modulate* usually lacks an effective lay replacement; it seems more often to call for a phrase or an entire revision of the point it appears in. But if your narrative is still on track when *modulate* rears its head, it is worth lingering over the passage to come up with good plain English wording that makes the idea clearer.

Factor. Readers know that a factor is something that contributes to a result and, when reading about common actions or events, can usually picture other factors that contribute and determine how important the contributions are. In science, the word *factor* ends up being fuzzy—even if the factor is given a name—when the contribution and its importance are outside the reader's knowledge. In most manuscripts that mention factors, the writer is just pointing out that the main contributor is not the only one. That backfires, however, because mentioning factors about which a reader can intuit nothing blurs the picture. A good principle is to be as resistant to *factor* as you are to *function*; a good solution is to search a dictionary or thesaurus for words that can sharpen the picture without your having to resort to fuller explanation. Straight-out synonyms, such as *building block, component,* and *member,* or related concepts, such as *part and parcel, aspect,* and *facet,* might be better—whatever will provide a sense of the category of contribution and a way to envision it.

Localize. In scientific texts, this word subjects readers to unnecessary heavy lifting. Like *prioritize* means "to make a priority," localize means "to make local"—for example, by adding crabs to the menu at a chain restaurant's seaside location. From context, a reader can figure out that the scientific version means either "pin down the location" or, in the passive "is localized," "found in a particular place," but reading slows down markedly when a term requires this type of sorting out. Lay readers do expect to slow down at times because of the subject matter, but lay-looking words with slightly different meanings tax readers' enthusiasm for the effort—especially if easy, clear expressions such as "pin down" or "found in" could say the same thing. The heaviest tax is paid when you most want the reader to be willing to follow a difficult but essential point.

Delineate. This is an example of a common word with scientific significance that can miss its mark. Its ordinary definitions—"to represent something by drawn or painted lines" (a waiting area, for example), "to outline something" (as lights on a runway), or "to spell out in detail"—are useful in discussing brain science. But some scientists also use the word to mean "to discover a structure or process." When discovery is the intended meaning, the writer must bring it out. Otherwise, the lay reader will not read it that way, because "to discover" is not one of the lay definitions of *delineate.* An even more common word susceptible to this particular misreading is *describe,* as when the writer is naming investigators who gave the first full account of a brain process or structure. Without knowing that describing a biological structure or process can be an advance in itself, the lay reader has no inkling of its actual importance.

Other words with term-of-art meanings in brain science, such as *represent,* have meanings that are different from lay usage but appear in contexts from which a reader can extract the scientific meaning. Ideally, on the theory of saving all heavy lifting for unavoidable jargon, you would not oblige a reader to go this extra length. Thus, if you can scrub your manuscript for these crossover terms, it will be better for doing so.

UNBLESSED USAGES

By "unblessed usages" I mean popular usages that lexicographers do not recognize. A famous former one is *hopefully*, which once strictly meant "in a hopeful manner." In the 1960s a new meaning started gaining popularity: "it is to be hoped; I hope; we hope." After thirty years, the authorities surrendered, and dictionaries added it as a second definition. (*Webster's* still carries a note justifying the usage as a "disjunct" that makes it "entirely standard.")

This section focuses on two words that many writers use in a way that lexicographers are still resisting. Most people draw the correct inferences from either usage—traditional or unblessed— in material about ordinary subjects, but they may be unable to do so in scientific material.

Problematic. The word means "uncertain, questionable, difficult to solve or decide," as in "The choice was problematic." It has no other formal definition. However, today, multitudes of writers use it to mean "troubled" or "beset by obstacles or glitches," as in "The law has been problematic since the day it went into effect." You might say, well, a law can be either questionable or troubled. And that is why *problematic* is problematic: you can't tell what the writer means without more information. Likewise, a lay reader cannot be sure whether a "problematic" brain study left unanswered questions or was error ridden. Using words only in their formally established senses is a good rule, but *problematic* seems like a special case: since using it to mean "troubled" is now so common, your correct use as "uncertain" may nonetheless be misunderstood. The better rule may be not to use it at all.

Like. The usage of *like* is contentious with grammarians, but the horse is out of the barn colloquially. In everyday speech and in a great deal of lay writing, *like* has unseated *such as.* Consider a hypothetical news item:

> Leaders like President Obama and Vladimir Putin will be at the UN this week.

Strictly speaking, *like* means "similar to, not the same as," so the sentence says only that heads of governments will be there. A careful writer would write, "Leaders *such as* . . ." because *such as* is inclusive—the presidents mentioned will attend along with other leaders. But we know what the news writer means, so we don't wonder about it.

But take a hypothetical sentence about the brain:

> The researchers are looking for neurotransmitters like serotonin and dopamine to get an idea of what the circuit does.

It is not clear if the writer is saying that serotonin and dopamine are two transmitters that the researchers are seeking or that they think the circuit uses transmitters similar to them. The reader would need to know a great deal of neuroscience to be able to distinguish. Since the chance of confusing the reader accompanies every misuse of *like* for *such as* in science writing, it only makes good sense to be a strict constructionist on this usage.

PRONOUNS

Pronouns, especially *this, that, it,* and *these,* have a way of becoming little fuzz balls. Because they seem innocuous, we tend to overlook them when we feel a narrative is losing clarity. Yet, very often, what a pronoun refers to is unclear, and, accordingly, the ideas that follow seem less logical or not as apparent to the reader as they do to the writer.

For example, I edited a manuscript that discussed addiction. After telling of studies finding a relationship between environmental cues and relapse, the writer described a study that found that most veterans who became addicted to heroin in Vietnam stopped using it when they returned home, as they'd left behind cues that promoted their addiction. The next sentence read, "This is how we know that addiction is a chronic disease."

In writing, as in everyday speech, *this* always refers to—or *should* refer to—what immediately precedes it, and the effect in this instance was startling. It gave the impression that the writer had attributed a major conclusion to a single finding. The writer was actually referring to all the evidence discussed in the preceding page and thus should have started the sentence, "Taken together, the studies of relapse have shown us that . . ."

More commonly, a pronoun slip is just confusing. Often *this, that,* or *it* follows a complex sentence containing more than one idea, so which idea the pronoun refers to is unclear. In other cases, the preceding sentence may set out only one idea but also list a series of things, and a pronoun beginning the next sentence may not obviously refer to either the series or the idea.

I saved these comments on pronouns for last, because monitoring pronouns is awfully hard when you are writing. Being aware that they can cause problems is useful, but it should not become a hang-up. And perhaps it might be reassuring to know that "What does [*this/that/it/these*] refer to?" is probably the copy editor's most frequent query.

PART THREE

SCIENCE AND STYLE

INTRODUCTION

SOME people think a good writing style takes talent. That's probably true in the same way it is for other pursuits—athletics, music, cooking, dancing, painting, photography, singing, or acting. A few people simply have a gift, but many more do something well, professionally or not, because it enticed them and they decided to acquire the skill. So, too, with writing.

Inspiration and passion help, but style emerges from how a writer understands and puts together the elements of writing. One is language—and it's a constant concern when science is part of the mix. But equally important are choices involving other basics: what to describe or explain, which analogies or anecdotes to use, how to organize the narrative, whether to paraphrase or to quote, and so on. Even though you make these choices from one line to the next, you need to start thinking about them ahead of time, as you gather materials and develop an outline.

Style is flexible, like attire: how we dress for a movie is different from how we dress for a dinner party. And we have personal constraints: just as some clothing styles feel better to us, so do some writing styles, but even then we choose with a view toward what's appropriate for the occasion. And finally, just as we generally stay dressed for wherever we go throughout the day, the style that's right for a project is consistent to the end.

Another analogy is how we visualize the people we expect to be with. Anticipating who will be reading and why leads to some choices and excludes others.

If you have a specific publication in mind for an article you want to write, the publication's editorial style is important. If you read it regularly, you already have a feel for how it handles subjects it publishes, but knowing that you enjoy a magazine is not the same as being prepared to write for it. To be sure that the way you want to write your article will fit the publication's style, review back issues with an analytical eye, and look especially for other articles involving science. Notice what style elements— for example, anecdotes or the lack thereof—contribute to your overall impression of the magazine and consider how such elements suit both your perspective and the type of information you want to include. You may find you need to shift your thinking (e.g., plan to dress up more or skip the blazer), or you may decide it's not the right publication for your piece at all.

The next seven chapters describe particular style choices that turn up in writing about science for lay readers. You've seen them all, but perhaps you haven't thought about them with respect to lay writing. Some may be tools that you've never needed—or that would even be undesirable—in writing for peers. Others are just alternative ways of doing what you already do.

8
SAYING
AND NOT SAYING

THIS chapter is mainly about the cognitive challenge to a scientist's writing style that Steven Pinker calls "the curse of knowledge," but it begins with a special problem that crops up in many scientists' writing for lay readers: forgetting to explain why things are important.

THE "WHY" PROBLEM

Even when scientific explanation is beautifully done, forgotten "why's" can throw the whole enterprise into a funk, making an article or book seem tedious or just too complicated. All kinds of academic subjects derail when authors forget the "why," but it is disproportionately damaging to science writing because most lay readers lack insights from other sources as they try to figure it out. Thus, a lawyer writing about a Supreme Court ruling can describe legal precedents and forget to say why they helped make the ruling important, and we at least know enough about the issues to guess the significance. With science, we lay readers seldom have enough routine exposure to make up for an author's failure to explain why, for example, a discussion of prions is significant in an article about Alzheimer's disease.

Forgetting the "why" seems particularly to afflict authors who craft beautiful, accessible descriptions of biological activities and features. My hunch is that while lovingly developing those details, the writer's own deep engagement makes their importance seem totally obvious or at least apparent. Another reason may be that interference from long experience writing for peers leads scientists to focus on facts without considering whether the reader can put those facts together without help. But when the reason for dwelling on particular details is obscure to a lay reader, the details are anchorless, and they become boring, confusing, or both. At worst, a kind of textbook syndrome descends on the narrative, and descriptions sit orphaned, as if an instructor will show up to explain what they mean.

Understanding the need to say why is a big part of solving the problem that Pinker described as going "back in your mind to the state you were in before you knew something and explain[ing] it to others." Time travel isn't the answer. The lay "why" is about how science supports the premise of an article or book. It is not a scientific question, such as "Why does one biological activity produce another?"

Realizing you've got a "why" problem is like Will Rogers's "first law of holes": if you find you're in a hole, stop digging. If you are writing a scientific passage and find yourself tortured as you try to turn details into clear English, you may be in a "why" hole. Stop and ask yourself, "Why am I including this information?" If it turns out that the point you are detailing is essential to your perspective, then ask exactly why it matters and then immediately capture that answer in your text.

The first payoff should be that seeing the "why" in black and white tells you to what extent the point connects to your main story line and thus how much detail you actually need in order to support the connection. And second, you will have written something you cannot afford to leave out: an explanation of why the science you describe matters to the idea at the heart of your article or book.

Once you're in the middle of writing, it can be tough to keep checking your bearings on the issue or perspective you set out to convey. Ideally, the time to ensure fidelity is before starting to write—by outlining your project in the form of sentences saying why your planned content connects with your premise. For example, in an article about the search for Alzheimer's treatments, your outline could read, "Section two: Discuss prions because . . ." Such an outline acts as both a reference if you find yourself in a "why" hole and a cheat sheet for vetting a completed first draft to make sure you took care of the "why's" you were expecting.

The best and most rewarding reason to sort out the "why" is that "why" is more enlightening to a reader than "what"— especially to one who reads to "talk about and share" or because "it makes me smarter." That's because, for a reader in a new and unfamiliar place, the "why" is intimately connected to you, the narrator and companion. Saying why a point matters brings out your views on the subject and thus offers a ready way for the reader to understand it. It also humanizes the reading.

David Mahoney, the late longtime chairman of the Dana Foundation who turned the foundation's focus to neuroscience, crystallized the question of why during the early years of the newsletter *BrainWork*. Whenever he read an advance copy of an issue he was dissatisfied with, he would call me and say something that boiled down to, "I have no idea why this is important." I've long forgotten individual instances and words, except for one line that he always used: "I want to know why neuroscientists get out of bed every morning." To him, the heart of a story was why the scientists cared about it. It was fundamental to his goal of making the public care about the science, too.

Similarly, when you are stepping up with a subject or issue that you feel should concern or excite your lay reader, the "why's" are the flesh and blood of your story.

SAYING AND NOT SAYING

In writing any given article or book, the crux of author's science-explanation problem is that most readers will lack discrete types of knowledge that underpin the science in the story. And the writer's challenge is not just to recognize knowledge a reader may lack, but also to decide whether it's necessary to supply it. Often it is not necessary, but occasionally failing to supply it is near-fatal.

What to say. In handling your science, deciding what to say begins with how "sciencey" you expect to be. If your perspective is "the science behind X," you know your reader is up for science as science—in contrast to an approach such as "strategies for beating stress," in which the science should be threaded into the narrative. For science as science, though, you still have to consider how far to go with what knowledge and concepts. You can expect this reader to have some basic information and ideas at the ready—though they're possibly pulled off a dusty mental back shelf—and to have noticed some relevant recent developments that attracted modest news coverage. Other facts and concepts that you bring to the telling will likely be brand-new, but you have the comfort of knowing that this reader takes pleasure in reading that calls for a little work.

It may seem counterintuitive, but writing science as science is where you (or your editor) may start thinking about Pinker's "curse of knowledge." It is incredibly easy to slip into seeing this reader as a passive vessel—a container into which you can pour X number of words of pure science—rather than as someone to whom you promised a perspective. Remembering the perspective is what saves you, because it causes you to take care to choose the details that are essential to (not just part of) that story.

For other approaches, sticking to the point of the story is easier, whether you are writing prescriptively, delivering an opinion, or discussing a philosophical or social issue. For these, you know where the science interfaces with your angle, and you know that neither you nor your reader wants it to be a science lesson. Hence, the point of view exerts more control; it's easier to select the science and the depth of explanation. For example, if you set out to write about how a promising Alzheimer's drug failed, you focus on why anybody thought it would work and what the failure revealed. You need just a few broad scientific strokes to communicate the big picture of the disease biology and all the other hypotheses about treating it.

Not saying. Whether an article or book is mostly science or contains just a little, not saying enough is as confusing to a lay reader as explaining too much, and it is harder for the writer to notice. You can see on the page if you are in overkill mode, but, by definition, omissions aren't there. The omissions that hurt usually involve a fact that everybody working in science knows. For instance, you don't need to tell a colleague why a brain image is only partly informative.

The solution is not to figure out what your reader doesn't know, but to imagine what your reader might *ask*. If you were in a conversation, what point might cause a listener to say, "Wait, why did they do that?" or "What did they want to know?"

Again, the perspective you've chosen (do I repeat myself?) is all-important. When you are letting it control your narrative, the reader's questions have a way of coming to mind more easily. In the brain image example, if you were talking to a neighbor about gains in stroke rehabilitation, you wouldn't dwell on the shortcomings of imaging; the value of nonimaging measures would be what matters. But if your perspective were the debate over brain images in criminal defense, you would know the lay media never mentions that research scans are aggregates, and you would have to add this key fact for a lay person to understand what might be wrong with using them.

When you think you may have failed to say something necessary, you may feel the floodgates of your training and experience opening up and start worrying that you will get swept away trying to bring the reader up to speed. To keep your balance, remember that a lay reader usually asks about the significance of a key point or concept, not the relationships of all the subordinate details.

9
ANALOGIES, SIMILES, METAPHORS, AND ANECDOTES

YOU don't need it, I know, but to be fastidious, here's a high school English flashback. The terms heading this chapter mean comparison (analogy), likening one thing to another (simile), a figure of speech using one thing to represent another (metaphor), and a short scene or story from personal experience (anecdote). The old saw about a picture being worth a thousand words applies to all of them.

ANALOGIES, SIMILES, AND METAPHORS

In neuroscience, some word pictures have been faithful standbys. The best-known analogy is numerical: the brain has more neurons than all the stars in the Milky Way. At least three similes have yielded scientific terms: dendrites (like the branches of a tree); hippocampus (like a seahorse); and amygdala (like an almond). And at least one neuroscience term is an outright metaphor: circadian clock.

From your reader's point of view, all such help is welcome. It has been a long time since Marc Raichle's group at Washington University in St. Louis published its famous PET images of the brain reading words, but now some imaging studies are targeting what goes on when people read literature. The findings will be interesting, but writers and habitual readers already know what matters: a reader visualizes what he or she is reading by transforming it from one-dimensional print into a 3-D experience. Good fiction depends on the reader's ability to lose him or herself in the "movie," but good nonfiction draws the reader into the reality portrayed in one-dimensional print, too.

Realizing that reading is participatory is salvation for a writer, too. It means that all of a reader's senses are ready to add to what the writer is offering. If you write that a brain is the consistency of tofu, the reader feels and sees it, and if you write that a neuron firing sounds like radio static, the reader hears it. In other words, you aren't lobbing dead word balls at a brick wall; an image that is vivid in your mind's eye will also be vivid in the reader's mind when you successfully put it in words.

You can even count on the reader to build a good image with hints—fragments of similes, so to speak. For example, you can say that an ion channel releases potassium into extracellular space, or you can say that the gates "spring open" and potassium ions "rush out to flood" the space outside the cell. The former wording imparts a scientific fact; the latter uses textured, visual words to show the reader something you've seen with your own eyes.

Analogies, similes, and metaphors are at home in any subject and any format for lay readers. By letting a reader apply the familiar to the unfamiliar, they encourage him or her to engage, and they make the subject more memorable. Since these images can clarify and sometimes replace scientific exposition, they are especially valuable when almost everything you need to say about the science is likely to be new to your reader.

Two other points about these devices are important. One is that they can be overdone. A word picture brightens the light around the idea or detail associated with it and thereby cues the reader to remember it. An undue proliferation of cues, however, can make it hard for a reader to determine what you want to matter most in your narrative.

The other point is that sometimes it may seem that you need a word picture, but actually you don't. If you are working on an explanation and a picture bubbles up from your imagination, give it a look and try some words. Chances are good you are recognizing a point on which the reader might not otherwise be clear, and the image will work. On the other hand, if you are writing a passage that you know will be difficult for the reader, but images and image-inducing words do not readily come to mind, straining to create a picture usually only produces a strained image. In this case, revising the passage to be simpler or more succinct is probably a better solution.

ANECDOTES

Anecdotes are glimpses. When they show science manifest in a patient or volunteer, or at work in the lab, they give real life to a scientific account. Consider the difference between saying, for example, that something "was thought to be" one thing but "found to be" otherwise, and mentioning that an unexpected finding began with a shipment of wrong-age mice and the scientists' decision to do the experiment anyway.

If an article needs to be shorter than, say, a thousand words, anecdotes must be brief, but a reader can fill in details from even small cues. For example, let's say you have room for a nod to science history and can mention that a rivalry between two famous nineteenth-century scientists in London grew so fierce that supporters of one shouted down the other at a dinner talk. That's all you need. The reader will construct the London dining room, the flickering candles, the shouting guests, and the startled speaker in one fell swoop. Depending on what other weight you've given the subject, the reader may see, hear, and feel the incident well enough to remember it—and the subject—long after reading your work.

Anecdotes have always been used in lay-magazine articles and have been common in newspaper writing for at least a century. More recently, in the 1980s, the anecdotal opener gained a foothold, and it has been the rage for works of every length ever since. It is now so typical for an article about a medical or disease-related science subject to begin with a patient's story that you could think moving or shocking readers to draw them in must be the first requirement. But it is not quite. It is just the most obvious way to appeal to a reader's desire to read an article that matters, that will be gripping and useful, or that will answer a major question, present a novel problem, explain a mystery, or put the reader in a place or situation he or she hasn't personally experienced. While an anecdotal opening typically suggests that one or more of these attractions is ahead, an expository opening can say what's ahead more directly. The expository opening is just harder to write interestingly.

Even though it's not particularly gripping, an expository opening may be best for subjects that have been prominent for a few years, such as Alzheimer's disease, PTSD, drug and alcohol addiction, depression, autism, and traumatic brain injury. Patient-centered anecdotes for these have been losing their power to compel, because a particular disorder's onset, course, and consequences are similar from one patient to the next. It's not that readers have grown insensitive to the plight of the people afflicted; rather, they suppose the familiar opening precedes equally familiar information. Since they remain interested in the problem, they look to something else—title, subtitle, pull-out quotes, pictures, quick skim of the text—to see if the story says anything new. In other words, a clichéd opening loses the ability to draw in the reader.

Many writers (or their editors) still feel they should lead articles about medicine or science with a sad story and do so even when the anecdote is barely connected with the subject. A June 2013 *New Yorker* article by popular doctor-writer Jerome Groopman begins with such an anecdote—a description of a man's decline and death from Alzheimer's disease. Its only point is that the man was the grandfather of a researcher coleading a major study of early Alzheimer's treatment. The rest of the article is about the debates over early treatment and whether beta-amyloid, tau, or something else causes the disease. In a shorter article on the same subject for a different publication, such a lead would misdirect the reader; the author would have to start another way and perhaps save the grandfather for mention a little later. But a 5,500-word article has room for loose connections, and the *New Yorker* has practically a brand-name stake in both digressive details and starting stories with a human-interest spin.

As a rule, then, what to treat anecdotally and when to do it should be closely related not only to how well the anecdote represents or advances the themes in your narrative, but also to what your reader is most likely accustomed to. The most important job of an anecdote is to put a human face on an idea; it's an example that doesn't begin with "For example."

Since science abounds with tales of surprise, setbacks, races to get to a finding first, serendipity, and so on, you have plenty of rich material to mine.

10
WHAT TO PUT FIRST

THE take-home message I want to deliver here is: Don't put first things first. That's right: *don't*.

Point-by-point style—consisting of first this, then this, then several more things, and, lastly, what it adds up to—is for recipes, detective stories, and suspense writing. In expository nonfiction, it is equivalent to bricklaying: piling up facts, each commanding attention with little or no reference to the meaning of the whole.

Historians and biographers sometimes write this way when they expect readers to generally know an era's major events and context, and the style ends up only boring. When the subject is scientific, however, point-by-point style is deadly. For a lay reader, trying to follow and retain one unfamiliar fact after another in an unfamiliar context is like feeling one's way down an unlit corridor.

Many scientists writing for lay readers try to provide guidance by starting an article or book with some positioning paragraphs or an introduction identifying the subject, what's important about it, and how it affects the reader. But then, when they arrive at the scientific material, they turn to point-by-point exposition, often laying out more than one set of facts before finally adding them all up. Then their editors beat them up, filling the margins with the repeated query, "What does this mean?"

From that description, you probably recognize what's wrong: the writing is journal style—introductory material, uninflected recitation of fact, and interpretation withheld until the end—leaving the reader to reach his or her own understanding of the details. And lay readers (and editors) rarely have enough general and contextual knowledge of the science to accomplish this task independently.

What to do? Lecturing, teaching, and writing up studies for publication are powerful conditioning, and stifling a style that has become natural and familiar is tough. A good instrument would be a simple, obvious formula for lay style, and of course there isn't one. But you can set two policies for yourself to accomplish a first draft with less struggle against the point-by-point habit.

The first, and maybe most helpful, is to outline the project in conceptual sentences only, while strictly resisting the temptation to list scientific details. Remind yourself that you know the science too well to need details in an outline and that what you want is to attend to the narrative. Cumulatively, the sentences will form a synopsis of your story, give you a picture of its proportions that can help suppress the point-by-point impulse, and, most important, keep you considering as you go along how the different parts matter. Here is a simple example for a hypothetical 1,750-to-2,000-word article about the outlook for Alzheimer's disease treatment:

(Announcement anecdote) In 2011, scientists adopted a new strategy against Alzheimer's disease.

The need for a change was urgent; the number of people at risk was rapidly growing.

Despite years of studying the disease, its cause remains uncertain, and existing therapies are few and weak.

Even when a cause is elusive, better treatment and prevention strategies can emerge, but they require a handle on the nature of the disease, and we now have that much.

We are surer of the biology, thanks to three pivotal discoveries, each of which gave us an important insight.

One let us better understand the pathology.

Another has shown how some people are more likely than others to be vulnerable.

And the third, announced in 2011, led to our shift in thinking about when treatment may help preserve memories and quality of life.

Taking advantage of these insights, new clinical strategies are under study.

In the 1990s, we thought we were only a decade away from conquering the disease, but found we were learning a lesson about predictions instead.

But the time was productive not only in clarifying the biology; it gave us findings associating exercise, social engagement, and education with cognition in aging. These findings, along with earlier diagnosis, will play into better strategies against the disease.

Our trip back to the Alzheimer's research drawing board turns out to be a good thing.

Outlining without details forces you to think only in the same terms as the reader: in terms of the consequences of the science. When you set details aside to work out a narrative, you set up the science for discussion in a natural and dynamic way. For example, the second sentence in the outline above refers to disease risk, which, on a bullet list of scientific points, might include education's possible protective effects. But by the time you reach the close of the article, a more relevant use for the education point appears, and that use might not come to mind via a bullet-list outline. Seeing your narrative structure in black and white enables you to choose the science that best illuminates each concept and to determine in what depth to discuss it, given the proportions of the story.

The other policy I suggest comes into play while writing a first draft. No matter how weird or awkward it might feel or look, when you turn to a scientific explanation, begin with *why* the science you will describe matters. You actually went through this process when you figured out what made you know you had a lay story to tell. Declaring the "why" immediately might not—probably will not—flow very well, but, with the reader having to attend closely to the science you describe, you need him or her to stay with you, to feel that it's worth it. You can revise and improve such transitions either while you're writing them or once you have your first draft. The important thing is to have a draft that is continually compelling in concept.

11
QUOTING AND
PARAPHRASING

MANY scientists write in a kind of go-it-alone state. They adhere so strictly to exposition that they overlook the advantages of quoting and paraphrasing. Both, however, are a writer's friends, because the words and ideas of others are so often interesting and useful. Historical comments—such as those from William James—can add weight and texture to a point; quoting a contemporary authority can underscore a consensus view or anchor a fact imported from another science. Cheeky quotes, such as the famous Woody Allen line that the brain is "my second-favorite organ," can remind a reader to relax. When someone else's words might be ideal but not quotable because of limited space or the need for permission, paraphrasing is the fallback.

Quoting and paraphrasing are very agreeable components of style. Their usage conventions are simple and flexible; they can fit smoothly into almost any writing format and length. Of course, using them purposefully is important; quoting only to have quotes makes a text verbose or muddled. Quotes have some pitfalls, too.

THE ADVANTAGES
It's helpful to think of quotes as evidence. Quoting provides support for an argument, for a way of looking at something, or just for a point that a writer would like to drive home.

In an argument, quotes are more interesting than a mere statement of a point that you plan to knock down. For example, instead of stating that many self-help gurus advocate a bad idea, quote the most famous guru, and then take apart the advocated idea.

Sometimes someone famously sums up a way of looking at something. Quoting that view is an excellent way to dispense with overview and get right to discussing specifics. A quote, such as one of a well-known axiom, also can help dispose of the need to state a basic concept and thus enable the writer to focus on its nuances.

When the significance of an idea is worth emphasizing, a quote can provide that emphasis. For example, writing about neurogenesis, a writer could merely write that no one thought it was possible until the 1990s. But quoting the view that prevailed for almost a century is a more emphatic way to bring home the magnitude of the change—whether the quote comes from Cajal or a widely used high school biology book of the 1980s.

Some basics. A few points about quoting are basic. First and obviously, quotes have to be attributed to their sources, but attributions should also be clear. Often, and not just in science writing, they're not. The commonest unclear attribution is that a named source said something, when, actually, the person wrote it. Using *said* instead of *wrote* is usually just careless, but some writers use it in a mistaken belief that using *wrote* in a work without notes means having to cite the source publication, title, and maybe the date in their text. But it is perfectly acceptable to make it *has written* or, if the source is dead, *once wrote.* The construct signals that the words per se are the significance, not the source document. The reader who would like to dig up more on those words is at least assured they might be available with an

Internet search.

The appropriate *said* or *wrote* is just one way of attributing. Characterizing the saying or writing can produce an interesting and informative attribution. Verbs such as *retort, speculate, declare, think,* and *note* can indicate a state of mind behind a source's words or strengthen the context. The need is still to indicate whether the words are written, but not necessarily with *wrote*—for example, "Charcot *retorted* in a later paper, '...'"

Another basic is to make sure the reader can see how the words serve as evidence in the context. For example, imagine a piece about pharmaceutical companies' retreat from psychiatric drug development. A writer might describe findings suggesting several targets for drugs, quote a company official about the firm's high hopes for one drug and its failure in trials, and point out that the firm's announcement that it would give up on developing psychiatric drugs was a scenario that grew increasingly common. In other words, a quote can rarely stand on its own; it needs to be clear why it's there.

Quotes are always embedded in a sentence, because a quote all by itself rarely makes sense. The most familiar way to embed a quote is a sentence that reads, "[Name] [said/wrote], '[quote.]'" Often, though, potential quotes are too wordy or include other ideas that will confuse the intended point, so the quote is cut down to the words that express the point, and the writer summarizes or paraphrases the rest. For example: "The researchers concluded the drug made no difference, writing that it was 'a wholly insignificant result.'"

Naturally, the point of the original must fairly relate to the use the writer makes of it. For example, if the researchers quoted were not writing about a drug that a pharmaceutical company gave up on, the quote could not be used as if they were—even if the researchers tested a similar compound for the same purpose. The writer would have to make the distinction and give the reason for quoting an outside finding.

Sometimes a good choice when embedding is to divide a quote, when one part or another better delivers the purpose for which the writer is using the quote. For example, this writer is using a quote to support the idea that a certain characteristic is a norm: "'A subset of the volunteers could not complete the task,' the researchers wrote, 'but a 95 percent majority completed it without difficulty.'"

Paraphrasing is essential when a promising quote is very important and irredeemably dull or jargony. A tenderhearted weakness of scientists is the desire to recognize groundbreaking work by a friend or a colleague they admire by quoting verbatim from that person's paper. And before the editor gets a look, the writer has shared the draft with others, including the friend or colleague. Oh, dear. How do you say, "This is awful?" Try to detach: some of your colleagues' papers are terrible reading, at least for lay people. Use your own language to salute the groundbreaker—and paraphrase.

THE PITFALLS

The one real peril of quoting is getting something wrong. So, just for fun, I took a closer look at the Woody Allen quote the way writers about the brain nearly always use it, which is, "As Woody Allen said, 'The brain is my second-favorite organ.'" It happens to be wrong in four ways—the citation, the wording, the punctuation, and possibly the attribution.

In the lay sense, the citation and attribution are both "Woody Allen said," which implies that, speaking as himself, Allen made the joke, perhaps during an interview. But the words were spoken[*]

---

[*] http://www.youtube.com/watch?v=ngizj5FIcjo

by a character Allen played in a 1973 sci-fi comedy. In the movie, *Sleeper*, he is Miles Monroe, owner of the Happy Carrot health-food restaurant. He gets cryogenically frozen, and two doctors thaw him out two hundred years later. The doctors warn him that if the government finds out that they thawed him, he and they will be destroyed. When he asks what "destroyed" means, they say his brain will be "electronically simplified." His horrified reaction: "My brain? That's my second favorite organ!"

Check out the difference between the original wording and punctuation and how we usually see it now.

But the attribution (in the sense of origination) is the most interesting gaffe. It's easy to think that, as writer-actor-director for the film, Allen conceived the line, but he cowrote *Sleeper* with his collaborator at the time, Marshall Brickman, another comedy writer, who had been head writer for Johnny Carson and Dick Cavett (and most recently wrote the musical *Jersey Boys*). Six years after *Sleeper*, Allen and Brickman went back to brain-as-organ in their collaboration *Manhattan*. In that film, Allen's character, Isaac "Ike" Davis, says, "You rely too much on the brain. The brain is the most overrated organ." So we have two possibilities: that Brickman wrote one or both lines and that neither line is Woody Allen's own mischievous take on the brain.

Plenty of careful writers (for example, Nancy Andreasen in *The Broken Brain*) have gotten this brain quote—and its citation— right. Though, apparently, neither Allen nor Brickman has ever griped about its decades of being something Woody Allen said. Why would they? Brickman has said their collaboration was a process of him and Allen taking walks and talking through the scripts. And, anyway, the quote fits Allen perfectly.

However, the situation might be different with a quote, casual or substantive, that was off base in one of the four ways that the

Allen quote is (citation, wording, punctuation, or attribution). And some characteristic lay styles and formats are quite prone to these pitfalls.

Citation mistakes are rare for scientist-writers, so I'll skip that. But attribution can easily go awry in writing for lay readers. This can occur when an article or a passage needs to be short. For example, when simplifying and compressing, trying to include nuances, and whittling down a quote, a writer might not notice that the resulting passage appears to show an investigator claiming both a finding and the principle that it was based on, although a different researcher developed the principle first. The risk for such slips is highest when a writer is between a rock and a hard place: a proliferation of names and nuances, though tedious, will be perfectly accurate, but a text is livelier when people *do* things, when findings and principles are in the active voice, and when quotes are used. All you can do is carefully vet the passage you wind up with.

When the subject is something other than science as science, it may help reduce the chance for error to treat findings as facts rather than calling them findings, and to go easy on detailed description to avoid inadvertently including a prior finding without attributing it properly. But giving facts without credit for their discovery can sometimes blot out a great research point. That is, some findings are not only facts but also so compelling that it is nearly impossible to mention them without attribution. For years, that was the case with anything about the amygdala—it would have been unthinkable to fail to attribute seminal facts to findings by Joseph LeDoux. In many other instances, though, while lay readers like knowing that real people did real work to establish facts, the "who," "how," and "what" often are irrelevant. Thus, starting down the path to attribution, with or without direct quotation, becomes a style issue: is the finding, or how it came to be, a fact interesting enough to enhance the story? If it is, attribution by name is necessary, not optional.

When it comes to wording and punctuating a quote, it's hard to go wrong with a source's words in black and white in front of you. Likewise, as with the Woody Allen quote, words taken from an audio or video recording will be accurate if you are viewing the original, and inflections and body language can guide punctuation. The potential problem arises in quoting unscripted speech—for example, a popular public speaker who makes a certain point, more or less the same way, in every talk. Punctuation can give the wrong inflection—for example, an exclamation point makes a remark close to a shout, when a speaker was actually being droll. The consequence may be no worse than an annoyed speaker who considered the punctuation a personality transplant, but more sensitive objections can involve context.

For example, consider the Pinker "curse of knowledge" quote that I've referred to several times. In the taped public appearances I've seen, he is making a point about cognition and urging his audience to be sympathetic to academics trying to write for the lay reader, but I've used it to contrast with what I think are desirable ways for scientist-writers to accomplish their task. He could, if he wanted, protest that my context makes his words seem like advice instead of empathy, whereas his full talks about writing offer plenty of actual advice. So which is it? I would say we both use his words the same way: to set up a perspective on a scientist writing for lay readers. His listeners and my readers are interpreting his words in the same way: it is hard for scientists to write for lay readers.

Scientific facts are more concrete than writing about writing, and that might seem to protect you from complaints about context. But it does not—especially when you are quoting from unscripted speech and sometimes when you are quoting from written material. Context can become an objection because writing for lay readers is interpretive; the meaning you assign to a fact can be, or seem to be, different from how the person you quote actually views it. Thus, even if a quote seems to fit your interpretation, you must recheck the speaker's or writer's context. It's an important safeguard: the talk or paper might spin the meaning a different way, perhaps different enough to make the quote inappropriate for your purposes.

12
WHAT WE KNOW AND WHEN WE KNOW IT

WITH room to discuss more than a few points in support of a premise, longer articles and books invite you to use plenty of detail, to show how one thing leads to another, and to get into peripheral matters influencing the subject. The opportunity to enrich your story can be a relief, but it is double-edged. Greater length sometimes leads writers to feel there is room for other readers, with adverse effects on the style of the writing. Then a problem develops, having to do with what we, the lay readers, know and when we know it.

When scholars—not just scientists—publish longer works for lay readers, colleagues and students read them, too, in search of insights in the field. Scholar-writers know this, and having extra room to satisfy their colleagues' interest often leads to thinking about them, not always intentionally, while writing. The upshot is the literary equivalent of multitasking, and the writer's divided attention takes a toll. It causes a drift in how the writer thinks about the lay reader and a shift in the focus. The writer still understands that the lay reader doesn't know much, but, in the "presence" of a more sophisticated reader, the goal becomes to put the lay reader more or less on equal footing with the sophisticated reader. The lay premise is no longer the writer's guide; observations, mechanisms, and fundamentals take over.

Here's what happens when multitasking breaks out: the first time a scientific detail—let's say, GABA—comes up, the writer hurries to attend to the lay reader's ignorance by carefully explaining GABA, its role in the nervous system, its mechanisms, and the specific mechanism that relates to the topic immediately at hand. The next time GABA comes up, a different action and relevance are under discussion, but, having mentioned the overall concept earlier, the writer assumes the lay reader now knows it and thus treats it familiarly. However, the reader focused only on the previous relevance, forgot the other actions mentioned, and very likely even forgot the term *GABA*. The narrative has just become obscure and fuzzy.

Some writers recognize that the reader may have forgotten a term introduced early in the text. Intending to be helpful, they write "as mentioned above" or "as described in chapter X." That makes it worse; it says, "Go look it up." Few lay readers are ready to go backward and search for information; most feel it is an imposition, because time for leisure reading is precious.

So the question is how to luxuriate in the richness of length without turning the reading into a chore for the lay person.

One way is to remember what it took for the sophisticated reader to become sophisticated and to be realistic about the lay reader. That should be easy. As a neuroscientist, you have the advantage of actually understanding what most writers only sense: that reading is a major user of working memory. If humans are lucky to remember more than seven unfamiliar digits, you know they won't recall very much about a hundred or so words of unfamiliar detail after reading a thousand more.

Since we humans need more going for us than abstractions bouncing around in working memory, other systems have to engage to help us remember. Sticking with GABA as the example, point number one is that, on the first mention, what lay readers need is the *opposite* of a tutorial. Although we might comprehend a good lay description of the mechanisms, we'll forget it, because mechanisms don't show us GABA in a way that impresses us with the scope and importance that indicate the term will be coming back in what we're reading.

The writer can do this by pushing us to see and feel that GABA is a major player in the brain's game. We attend more to metaphors such as "workhorse"; we readily register a neurotransmitter's action when it is associated with things that are easy to visualize, such as "calms the nerves." We are comfortable reading that, whatever GABA is doing on the first mention, it's only the first important thing we'll be reading about in the transmitter's repertoire.

The essential thing for the writer to keep in mind is that everything we will need to know about GABA's action need not be said at once. If mechanisms dribble out while we are being impressed with what the neurotransmitter accomplishes, we'll follow and digest those mechanics better. On the second and other future mentions, those initial cuing references are your tool. We will have assigned tangible meaning to them—"Oh, right, the workhorse, the calming transmitter"—and should be ready for the new associations.

13
MASKED MEN AND UBOs

PEOPLE recognize legendary figures without seeing their full names. Something about Caesar, Washington, Napoleon, Churchill, Hamlet, Little Nell, Uncle Tom, Gatsby, Michelangelo, Van Gogh, Picasso, Galileo, Newton, Edison, Einstein, Freud, Watson, and Crick managed to touch humanity beyond the era or issue that first made them prominent. Highly educated people have studied still more figures, and professional literature is sprinkled with locutions such as "Spinoza would have recognized today's . . ." or "As Doe predicted . . ." Professional readers know who these people are, but such important names may only ring a bell, at best, with less sophisticated (or specialized) readers.

Erudite one-name and other unexplained references are a style I call "masked men and UBOs" for their befuddling effect on lay readers, who by definition live outside a science's usual frames of reference. Like mystified townspeople in old movies, the readers pause to wonder what happened, shrug, and move on, skipping over whatever these references were meant to convey.

MASKED MEN
Since they don't want readers skipping lines, scientist-authors almost always respond well to editorial queries asking for first

name and identification. Back comes the full name with some words to pull off the person's mask—to situate the person in his or her time, place, institution, and area of significance. Lead researchers turn out to have interesting names or to have done their work in interesting places; faintly recognized names turn out to have reshaped a field of study. Often, too, making the identification prompts the writer to sharpen up something about the point of the reference, and sometimes thinking about the name gives rise to a quick digression that adds color to the narrative or more interest to the point. This makes thorough identification a benefit to the writing—not just an onerous responsibility of trying not to flummox the reader.

Less often, the editorial query for more information causes the name in question to disappear, along with the point that prompted its use. This happens because, when adding the first name and working out the identification, the author realized that the whole point was more abstruse or less relevant than he or she had been thinking. The problem is that simple deletion may wind up weakening the narrative.

Masked-man references are not the same as slipping into tutorial mode. They come more with "why" writing than with "what" writing—when the text brings the reader into the writer's own frame of reference, versus kicking him out—and usually when the narrative is going well. (That's why the editor is querying only for identification.) Opting for deletion solves the problem of a less than stellar point, but the writer was probably right about needing something like the thinking that the reference represented. Then the writer finds it necessary to make a similar point in a different way, which means more writing to make sure that the "why" discussion still has all its legs.

The best preventive against masked men is to make a habit

of giving full names and capsule identifications in the first draft rather than waiting for an editor to ask. This habit solidly supports the narrative, especially if thoughtful identification provides an unexpected boost, and, if identification happens to show that a point isn't really apropos, it saves writing (and editing) time and effort. That is, it saves not only time spent on a wrong point but also time spent reconsidering and writing a substitute passage later, with publication right around the corner. What could be better than that?

UBOS

UBOs are unidentified biological objects, and, like UFOs, they turn out to be things we've seen before, but not often, or in a different light. We encounter the UBO in longer, denser articles and in books, because it's a reference to a previously explained scientific detail and the writer doesn't remind us of the earlier explanation.

To notice and avoid UBOs is part two of my earlier advice to emphasize tangible, easily visualized qualities of a biological detail, such as GABA, when introducing it. Having set good cues in the first discussion and gone on to other subjects since then, the writer needs to word the new reference in a way that activates those cues. A technical term such as *GABAnergic* can't do that by itself. It can cue the name, GABA, but a reader's sense of familiarity depends on evoking something of the coherence the writer provided on the first mention.

Since that entails both reminding us readers and setting us up for a new aspect to be revealed, it can seem complicated. For example, it's easy to remind readers that GABA is a workhorse— you just call GABA a workhorse again—but using an earlier cue like "calming" and then getting into GABA's being excitatory in development would seem more confusing than clear. Actually, it is easier, because the new aspect is more interesting by virtue of being so different from earlier cue. The writer only needs to recheck what he or she wrote the first time and be sure to write that the new aspect is the opposite. In other words, remember what you wrote, decide what will be different in what you're writing now, and point it out.

You might imagine that two or three or more featured appearances and explanations of a biological feature ought to be enough for us to get it. Don't count on it—at least not in terms of mechanisms and biological relationships. After twenty-plus years, I know GABA, but nothing like you know GABA; I had to hit Wikipedia to confirm everything I just wrote about it. But we *will* understand the importance and significance of the biological features you write about, and these are the main things you want us to know. Oh, and we'll end up with proprietary pride in having learned them and gratitude to you.

14
VISUAL STYLE

PEOPLE form an impression of an article or book without reading a word of it; we feel or lose interest based on a quick visual scan. Thus, as soon as they decide to write for lay publication, most authors start to think about titles, formatting, and art—the visible aspects of style. Specifically, some writers are thinking about how similar subjects look in magazines or books, how other articles or books made a good impression, and what the writers' friends and colleagues might approve of.

Those considerations are useful, but the best way to think about visible style is based on what I have been harping on: what you intend to say and who you see as your reader. For one thing, certainty about substance and reader is good self-defense, because editors start throwing their weight around when it comes to what they feel a reader's first impression will be. Lucky (or brilliant) is the writer who ends up with the same title that was on the manuscript, and more than one writer has been surprised upon seeing the first galleys of an article or book. If what's in your manuscript harmonizes with its visual impression, the editor (inevitably) will still suggest changes, but they should be tweaks rather than a remodel.

An even more important reason to stick with your substance/reader formulation, though, is that titles, text, and art, which seem like independent or even mechanical choices, relate closely to how you write while you are drafting. Any advance thinking you do about the visual style should steer clear of preconceiving what it should look like, because your writing itself will generate appropriate visual requirements. Which might be another way of saying, "Form follows function."

TITLES

Titles are short messages, and a prospective reader takes them as such. Readers respond to the subject or theme put forward by the main title and gain understanding from the subtitle and the progression of section or chapter titles. But until a manuscript is in final editing, these elements have another role, as messages from the writer to the writer saying, "Here's where I want my story to go."

Working Titles. The phrase "working title" looks like "sorta, maybe, what the title might be," but it is more than that. Once struck by an idea, the writer works out the idea and the natural reader, and the premise emerges from bringing idea and reader into focus. The working title expresses and anchors both.

For example, throughout the writing of his 2012 book, *The Age of Insight*, Eric Kandel's working title was *Uncovering the Unconscious*, reflecting his neuroscientific idea and a psychology-minded lay reader. I doubt that any other title could have kept the writing on track, because he was drawing from a great trove of non-neuroscientific material—art, literature, medicine, and psychology in late-nineteenth- and early-twentieth-century Vienna—and passing it all through the lens of present-day neuroscience. Nor would the published title have been as good a working title, because it alludes to both the era and the scientific perspective. It is a brilliant final title, but its dual focus would have thwarted a working title's anchoring purpose, and it might have thwarted the writing as well.

In short, the working title works for the writer. It is most serviceable when it captures the premise as well as the writer can express it and keeps the writer aware of the reader. It is not very helpful if it only has a snappy ring or seems commercial. Nor does form matter. It can be a whole sentence or a fragment and can take an active form using a verb or a static one consisting of nouns. One writer may feel best positioned with a working title that leaves wiggle room, as *Uncovering* left room for Kandel to keep thinking of both the exploratory subtleties of the earlier era and modern neuroscience findings. Another writer might want to keep the idea constrained due to potential controversy and decide that nouns will suit that purpose—like this one from when working titles were actual titles: *On the Origin of Species by Means of Natural Selection, or the Preservation of Favoured Races in the Struggle for Life.*

The one wording requirement for a working title to be a good anchor is that the title pick up on the way you expect to handle the subject for the reader you envision. That is, if you are thinking of the readers of, say, *Prevention* magazine, you'd make it "The Gene You Don't Want in Alzheimer's Disease" as opposed to "The Apolipoprotein E Phenotype in AD." Of course, if you come up with something like "Fifty Shades of GABA," I can't help you.

Subtitles. Editors are great perpetrators of subtitles, and the reading public is conditioned to expect them. They're now common with articles, even not very long ones, and almost all nonfiction books. Because their main purpose is to explain otherwise mystifying titles, the writer with a good, self-explanatory working title usually doesn't bother with a subtitle until the writing is done.

But many writers start out with an attractive, mysterious title that they feel reflects the theme of their idea and will appeal to the intended reader, even if it doesn't reveal the perspective they're writing from. That's sometimes enough, and the writing turns out clear and well focused. Other times, the theme can't quite guide the writing, and the narrative wanders. That's when a subtitle can be helpful, by articulating a premise to channel the narrative and acting as a working title.

Subsection and chapter titles. When published, many articles and books don't have either of these types of titles. But in a first draft of a long article or a book, subsection and chapter titles can be useful as mini working titles. You can relax and write and, when done, check back with them to see if you've nailed what you thought you needed to say. If you want or will be able to have them in publication, then you can edit these mini working titles to do their message-sending duty to the lay reader.

To me, the intention to have subsection or chapter titles is the reason for a really good synoptic-sentence outline ahead of starting to write. Since you may be expected to show an outline to an editor, the sentence form shows you telling a story, not just identifying chunks of content. But preparing the outline that way is a bigger benefit to you, in the form of a great writing reference. By "reference," I don't mean the editor will hold you to it; most manuscripts turn out different from the original outline. Rather, the sentence form can help a first draft two ways.

First, in the thick of writing, it's easy to lose track of what you planned to say next. When you check the story as it unfolds in the outline, you may find you've gone off spontaneously in a different direction, one that you like but that eventually will have to come back to other points you intend to include. Seeing the outline prompts you to think about handling the new direction before it gets out of hand. Second, when you arrive at a section that you foresaw in the outline, the sentence encapsulating it may give you, or may trigger, the wording you need for the section subhead or chapter title. Also, for a scientific section, the wording can remind you how you planned to spell it out for the lay reader.

TEXT BREAKS, INDENTATION, AND FOOTNOTES

Since lay readers dread being attracted to something scientific and finding it too dense to understand, an article or book can be a gem of lay writing, yet lose readers because of how the text looks. Fortunately, you can make sure that doesn't happen by noticing the visual style you're setting up. Good use of text breaks, indentations, and footnotes can signal to readers that they can handle the weight and pace of the story—and, by implication, the information.

Text breaks. Because text breaks give us welcome brief pauses, the familiar advice is to avoid long paragraphs that can make us feel we are trudging through a text. Visually, too, the absence of long paragraphs is generally a good signal, suggesting a more relaxed writing style. But breaking up scientific passages for the sake of appearance can backfire because they sometimes make the text appear more technical rather than less. That is, a scanning reader notices the higher number of technical paragraphs, and this wouldn't happen if scientific passages were allowed to run a little long.

A wonderful example of good paragraphing in a book is *The Emperor of All Maladies: A Biography of Cancer* by Siddhartha Mukherjee. His nontechnical paragraphs are usually fewer than a hundred words; those describing studies and findings are often twice as long. In newspapers and magazines, both print and online, the use of columns creates pressure for short paragraphs, but letting scientific ones run longer remains a good idea; the overall visual message will be of more nontechnical material.

That said, paragraphing has to make inherent sense. Since each paragraph deals with a topic, you can't arbitrarily cut one off because it is getting long, but you can ask why it is long. You may find it has become verbose or too technical, that it has more than one topic in it, or all of these.

A valuable text break is the line-space break—an extra blank line between passages. This is a print feature, and magazine editors prefer it as a way to create sections without subheads. Many book editors also use it to separate sections, with only a typographic symbol at the center of the blank line. If a book has subheads, a line-space break signals a change of aspect within a subsection—that is, the new aspect is still part of the topic indicated by the subhead but is different from the aspect that preceded it. Since a proliferation of subheads can make a text look jumpy, or too broken up (as a textbook might be), the line-space break is a good loosening-up tool for closely related topics that you can combine under one subhead.

Section and chapter closings are obviously text breaks, and the prospective reader's cue about content comes from the next subhead or chapter title. But the absence of a new title or the presence of a very interesting one prompts our attention to the lines before and after the break, and that fact calls for a cautionary word about transitions when you open and close.

A dry summary closing, or an opening that pronounces the next topic, does you no favor. Transitions should be interesting in the storytelling sense and should use expressive language. For example, notice the language Mukherjee uses when closing one subsection and opening the next in his chapter about cytotoxic therapies (the italics are mine):

> To produce a cancer remission one did not need a *toxic, indiscriminate* cellular *poison* (such as cisplatin or nitrogen mustard).

***

> If prostate cancer could be *starved to near death by choking off* testosterone, then could hormonal *deprivation* be applied to *starve* another hormone-dependent cancer?

Compelling language on both sides of breaks suggests that a reader will find the rest of the book compelling, too.

Indentation. Long quotations read better when separated in the text by making them indented paragraphs or excerpts. Since indentation makes a quote stand out, it also becomes a visual style telling the reader to pay attention and indicating that the quote is particularly significant. This has implications for your choosing to quote at length. One is that the quotation needs to be worthy of the visual distinction; the writing should be at least as readable as yours and the content self-evidently interesting. The corollary, if the substance of the quotation is scientific, is that it should be in well-written lay language. A long quotation from a scientific paper, even one reporting a profound finding, is sure to be more technical than a lay reader will understand. And if the reader has not yet decided to read, his or her natural assumption will be that the regular, unindented text is probably also hard to fathom.

Footnotes. Magazines for a general readership don't use footnotes, but some special-interest consumer publications—on health, for example, especially online—accept a very small number, as endnotes, with articles by doctors and scientists. The difference comes from the fact that notes look academic; publishers for a general readership emphasize the leisure aspect of reading, while publishers of special-interest consumer magazines know their readers like the sign of authority that notes impart. Similarly, when a book has a wide readership potential, endnotes are welcome (even plenty of them), but in-text numbering is not. If you are writing for the general-interest reader and the publication you are eyeing does not use notes, you'll have to leave them out. (But it is a good idea to save your references until the editing is over; they may be helpful for answering editorial queries.)

ART

Art is the editorial word for any visual depiction—photo, drawing, scan, graph, or table—and it is the element of visual style with the most influence on a reader's perception of how an article or book handles its subject. It also can influence how the writer writes.

Many writers gather potential art early on, when preparing to write, but, except for explicitly educational articles or textbooks, the writing usually will be better without considering art at all. The expectation of using art, particularly images such as scans and drawings, promotes more technical writing and weakens the incentive to use language to bring ideas to life. If a writer relies too much on an art scheme, the text can become overloaded, with art-driven details crowding out or competing with concepts that readers otherwise could readily understand and absorb.

Depending on the subject and reader you have in mind, making an early commitment to specific art also can be a waste of time and effort. Most general-interest print publications want little or none; they want the author's writing to be good enough that any art is reinforcing or enhancing rather than explanatory. The preference for words to tell the story is the same for online articles, but magazine sites do offer the reader art separately, to access by choice. Special-interest consumer publications, both print and online, are more amenable to displaying art along with text, but only to the tune of a handful of images. On the other hand, book editors reflexively shrink from technical art, including graphs and charts, as they know how little it takes for a book to start looking like a textbook. They are more generous about conventional images (a category that some editors feel now includes colorful brain scans).

The best way to harmonize manuscript and art is to stay away from art research and decisions while writing and, when images come to mind, to interrogate them: are you here because I'm having trouble expressing myself? Because I'm getting into too much detail? Because I'm a scientist? If the answer is that the image visually expresses what you have successfully said in words and looks good too, it should get a note in text for later review. Art that seemed compelling in the heat of a writing moment may look less so on cooler reflection, and finishing the draft before selecting any art lets you assess both individual passages and the overall manuscript for the right images. Going about it this way may also increase the likelihood of being happy with the publisher's handling of your choices, because, although editors do glance at your art while editing the manuscript, they will suspend judgment about it until the editing is done.

The power of art to shape the reader's experience is implied in the publishing expression "art program," which refers to a manuscript's proposed art and its editorial effect, specifically and cumulatively. All kinds of aspects are believed to shape a reader's perception of a published article or book: how clearly the art speaks for itself, its quality (image resolution, for example), what kind of caption it requires to be understood, and whether the idea in the associated text is worth illustrating at all. While it feels as if the art should be just one part of telling your story, it is inevitably the most direct visual message to the reader about who you have written for. Getting that message right is important.

ONE MORE THING

A completed first draft is a great feeling, especially if you're one of those writers who constantly revises while writing in an attempt to get everything right from the start. Nevertheless, you need to be willing to make more revisions after finishing.

It's a given that your editor will have many suggestions, but upon completing a draft and before submitting it to the editor, one of the most valuable things you can do is to find a few lay readers to review it. Have them tell you what they didn't understand—and, if they can, why. Many scientists share a draft with some colleagues, but few colleagues are good at seeing a draft as a lay reader would see it. After all, they have their own sophisticated take on the science, and it's hard to detach, whether reading something picked up at the newsstand or a friend's lay writing.

Scientists who write for nonscientists get lay feedback in all kinds of ways, but recruiting relatives, and sometimes relatives' friends, seems to work well. They ask their consultants to read the draft on paper with a pencil or pen nearby and mark where they have any difficulty with the narrative, whether they become confused or just don't understand the language, and to mention, if possible, what gave them a problem with it. This is a good way to ask for comment, because knowing that a passage isn't clear is easier than recognizing what caused the problem. Some people can articulate the cause very effectively, while others can only pinpoint where they got lost. The best thing about such feedback is that it is as close as you can get to an actual reader before you turn your draft over to your editor. (If the editor happens to be a scientist too, the lay consultants' feedback will be that much more crucial.)

Your lay readers' feedback, if you tap a few people, may be contradictory, since people differ in how they handle new information. What will be helpful to you is simply getting and reviewing all the questions or comments that occurred to people reading it with fresh eyes. This feedback shouldn't send you into robo-revision, however. People can be wrong about what puts them off what they read. The reason can be anything from not being very interested in the perspective to not caring for the voice.

A first draft is first because it will be revised, but you are the last word on, and best judge of, the right revisions. The good thing about readers' feedback is that it helps loosen your ties to the first draft so that you reread more objectively and make changes more willingly and with more detachment. The effect will be on your weakest writing—not your strongest.

Good luck!

OTHER READING

About readers

Baumer, Eric; Sueyoshi, Mark; Tomlinson, Bill; "Exploring the Role of the Reader in the Activity of Blogging," Published in Proceeding, CHI '08 Proceedings of the SIGCHI Conference on Human Factors in Computing Systems, pages 1111–1120; ACM New York, NY, USA ©2008. Online: http://ericbaumer. com/wp-content/uploads/2012/10/chi1132-baumer.pdf. "Bloggers and Readers Blogging Together: Collaborative Co-creation of Political Blogs," by the same authors, focuses on relationships between readers and bloggers in the context of political blogs (an open access article): http://link.springer. com/article/10.1007%2Fs10606-010-9132-9/fulltext.html

Peck, Abe; "The Third Way to Media Success," *Pacific Standard*, Nov–Dec 2010. Online edition: http://www.psmag.com/ media/the-third-way-to-media-success-23575/

"Report: Social Network Demographics in 2012," Royal Pingdom; posted in Tech blog on August 21, 2012, by Pingdom. Online: http://royal.pingdom.com/2012/08/21/ report-social-network-demographics-in-2012/

Shore, Jennifer; "Twitterature: 14 Connected Authors Worth Your Follow," Mashable.com, Sep. 14, 2012. Online: http://mashable.com/2012/09/14/twitter-writers/

"State of the Media: Social Media Report Q3"; Nielsen/ NM Incite, 2011. Online: http://www.nielsen.com/us/en/ reports/2011/social-media-report-q3.html

Stanford University, "MRI Reveals Brain's Response to Reading." Futurity, Sep. 10, 2012. Online: http://www.futurity. org/science-technology/mri-reveals-brain%E2%80%99s-response-to-reading/

About writing

"Writing and Submitting an Opinion Piece: A Guide." The Earth Institute, Columbia University, rev. Feb. 2010.

Blum, Deborah; Knudson, Mary; Henig, Robin Marantz; *A Field Guide for Science Writers: The Official Guide of the National Association of Science Writers,* Second Edition. Oxford University Press, USA, 2005. 336 pages.

Graves, Robert; Hodge, Alan; *The Reader over Your Shoulder: A Handbook for Writers of English Prose.* Random House, Second Edition, 1979. 290 pages.

kdel09; "Carl Zimmer's Advice for Aspiring Science Writers." Sciopic (blog), Jan. 29, 2013. Online: http://sciopic.wordpress. com/tag/science-writing/

Leite Vieira, Cássio; "The Little Manual on Science Communication: A summary." SciDevNet, 2008. Online: http://www.scidev.net/global/communication/practical-guide/ -the-little-manual-on-science-communication-a-summ.html

Safire, William; *Fumblerules: A Lighthearted Guide to Grammar and Good Usage.* Doubleday, 1990. 153 pages.

Scharf, Caleb A.; "In Defense of Metaphors in Science Writing." *Scientific American* blog, Life, Unbounded, July 9, 2013. Online:

http://blogs.scientificamerican.com/life-unbounded/2013/07/09/in-defense-of-metaphors-in-science-writing/

"Write for Us" (Submission Guidelines), BrainBlogger.com: http://brainblogger.com/call/

Index

A

B

C

W

About the Author

Jane Nevins, editor in chief emeritus of Dana Press, began her career in Southern California as a newspaper and magazine writer and editor and later moved to the East Coast, where she served as director of Audience Relations for the Voice of America and was a speechwriter for Secretary of Labor Ann McLaughlin and Secretary of Housing and Urban Development Jack Kemp. She began working with the Dana Foundation in 1990. She is the author of *Turning 200: A Bicentennial History of the U.S. Constitution* (Richardson & Steirman, NY; 1987).